Inside Role-Play in Early Childhood Education

How do children respond to role-play in school?

How can role-play be meaningful and relevant to children's learning?

Young children's preoccupation with role-play is widely recognised, and those aged from three to five years engage in it more than in any other kind of play; it can help them to develop social competence and to explore language and ideas about the world.

Based on extensive research, and grounded in everyday classroom practice, this book addresses important questions about play in the early childhood curriculum. Throughout, the authors present the child's perspective on play in schools and argue firmly against a formal, inflexible learning environment for young children. The book presents children's views on role-play alongside examples of classroom practice. It explores issues such as:

- Will structuring role-play replace children's own attempts to create scenarios that grow out of their interests and relationships?
- Has an overemphasis on subjects like literacy and numeracy eclipsed the important processes inherent in children's social play?
- How we can ensure that provision for role-play fully benefits all young children?

The issues raised in the book apply widely to international debates about the role of play in early childhood education. It will prove an invaluable book for students on primary education and early childhood studies courses at undergraduate and postgraduate level. Academics, researchers and course leaders will also find this book a compelling read.

Sue Rogers is Senior Lecturer in Education at the Institute of Education, University of London, UK.

Julie Evans is Senior Lecturer in the Sociology Department of the University College Plymouth St Mark and St John, UK.

Inside Role-Play in Early Childhood Education

Researching young children's perspectives

Sue Rogers and Julie Evans

Routledge
Taylor & Francis Group

LONDON AND NEW YORK

First published 2008
by Routledge
2 Park Square, Milton Park, Abingdon, Oxon, OX14 4RN

Simultaneously published in the USA and Canada
by Routledge
270 Madison Avenue, New York, NY 10016

Routledge is an imprint of the Taylor & Francis Group, an informa business

© 2008 Sue Rogers and Julie Evans

Typeset in Garamond by
GreenGate Publishing Services, Tonbridge, Kent

Printed and bound in Great Britain by
TJ International Ltd, Padstow, Cornwall

Every effort has been made to ensure that the advice and information in this
book is true and accurate at the time of going to press. However, neither the
publisher nor the authors can accept any legal responsibility or liability for any
errors or omissions that may be made. In the case of drug administration, any
medical procedure or the use of technical equipment mentioned within this
book, you are strongly advised to consult the manufacturer's guidelines.

British Library Cataloguing in Publication Data
A catalogue record for this book is available from the British Library

Library of Congress Cataloguing in Publication Data
A catalog record for this book has been requested

ISBN10 0–415–40496–7 (hbk)
ISBN10 0–415–40497–5 (pbk)
ISBN10 0–203–93030–4 (ebk)

ISBN13 978–0–415–40496–9 (hbk)
ISBN13 978–0–415–40497–6 (pbk)
ISBN13 978–0–203–93030–4 (ebk)

Contents

Acknowledgements

Our thanks must go first and foremost to the children and the adults who participated in this project. They remain anonymous, yet gave their time and energy to the project so generously. We are indebted to them all.

There are many others who helped in the production of this book. First, the study would not have been possible without funding from the Economic and Social Research Council (award no: R000223885), nor without the help of Professor Peter Woods, co-applicant with Sue on the original proposal, whose wise advice and incisive comments on drafts of our various papers were always gratefully received by us both. We conducted the study while we were both based at the University of Plymouth, so thanks must also go to colleagues there for support provided. In the writing of this book, our thanks must go to our colleagues at the Institute of Education, London, and the University College Plymouth: St Mark and St John. Julie is particularly grateful for institutional support via the Promising Researcher scheme which enabled her to develop papers that eventually contributed to the book. Many other colleagues have contributed in some way to this book, but special thanks go to Professor Alex Moore for commenting on one of the chapters, to Dr Colin Dawson who offered support to the project at every step of the way, and to Dr Rachel Torr who has cajoled, supported and badgered Julie to 'just get on with it'. Our thanks also to Alison Foyle at Routledge and to the production team for their efficiency and flexibility in the latter stages.

We have reported on the ESRC project data in articles published in *Educational Research* and the *European Early Childhood Education Research Association Journal*. We are grateful to the publishers (Taylor & Francis) for permission to reproduce material.

Last but not least, our thanks must go to our families and friends who remained patient throughout and endured considerable neglect in the later stages of the book. In particular our love and thanks go to our mothers Rhoda Langley (née Faraday) and Elizabeth Margaret Evans (née Behennah) who have endured our long absences.

Introduction

> Some things about children become so familiar to us that we lose sight
> of how remarkable they are – and lose sight too, of how little we
> understand the processes that underlie developmental achievements.
>
> (Hobson, 2002: 5)

The book is not about *how* to do role-play. Rather this book sets out to describe
how young children, in their first year of school, experience and find meaning
in role-play, and in so doing it aims to illuminate some of the key issues, tensions and dilemmas in developing a pedagogy of play. The discussion draws on
material collected in a year-long ethnographic study of children's role-play in
three reception classes in England, funded by the Economic and Social
Research Council. It was a real privilege to work with both the children and
adults who participated in the study, not least because it enabled us to get
'inside' children's role-play, but also because it gave us an opportunity to
understand better some of the pedagogical issues that surround play in early
childhood education. Moreover, the project raised important questions in our
minds about current ways of schooling young children in England. A further
consideration that arose in the course of the project was the challenge for us as
adults and researchers of working with children in an authentic way that
enabled them to share with us their views about play. So to a considerable
extent, this book is also about the process of research and some of the tensions
and dilemmas with which we were confronted. We hope by discussing this
process in detail we will both encourage and inform others who may wish to
pursue research on young children's perspectives.

The study was small in scale and specific to the English educational system. Nevertheless, we believe that many of the issues raised in the book apply
more widely to international debates about the role of play in early childhood
education. We hope also that practitioners will find something here that res-
onates with their own classroom experience.

There was nothing distinctive or remarkable about the three classrooms in
which we carried out the research. Indeed, they were in many ways remarkably

typical of reception classes in the UK more generally in terms of the nature of the activities available to the children, classroom organisation, the day-to-day routines and the warm and caring relationships evident between adults and children. However, our time spent in the project classrooms convinced us that there is something truly remarkable about the activity we call role-play, not simply because it integrates a range of skills and processes unique to human learning, but also because the children, most of whom were aged four at the time, told us that it is one of the things they liked most about school. At the same time, we believe that the significance of role-play in young children's lives is sometimes overlooked by educators and policy-makers alike, precisely because it is so common an activity in early childhood. The teachers too shared innovative and creative practices with us in spite of working in quite difficult and demanding circumstances.

Underpinning the discussion presented here are two key observations to which we refer often throughout the book. The first of these is that being four is a particularly important time for children, when a number of lifelong capacities appear to converge: 'they know that other people have minds, that the world exists independent of their subjective reality and that words have meaning' (Gopnik *et al.*, 1999: 133). Of course, it can be argued that any time in a human's life is potentially important, so we ask readers to indulge us here for a moment. Our point is that most four-year-olds in the UK currently attend school, entering the so-called reception classes of primary schools. While new curriculum frameworks in England and Wales such as those framing the Foundation Stage (and the soon to be implemented Early Years Foundation Stage) endorse playful and active experiences for reception-age children similar to those recommended for their nursery peers, our experience coupled with findings from several other recent research studies show that this is not always the case in practice. A key aim in this book is, therefore, to raise the profile of this group of children, to emphasise *being four* rather than *becoming five*.

Our second observation derives from sociocultural perspectives that describe learning as socially and culturally situated and that acknowledge children's agency in their experiences. Research internationally has noted that increasingly role-play in early childhood pedagogy is valued mainly for the ways in which it reproduces and rehearses the expectations of society (Guss, 2005), emphasises social realism rather than the transformative quality of play (Brogstrom, 1997) and focuses on curriculum subjects rather than the qualities that children bring to bear on it (Bergen 2002). Immediately we can see how a tension between children's play and perceptions of curriculum and pedagogy arise. As we will see in Chapter 1, research undertaken in the UK has noted dichotomies between play and work and between adult-intensive and child-initiated activity. Play may be used in the instrumental or educational sense, in order to promote certain learning outcomes in early childhood settings. However, many other important features of role-play, not least its potential as a sociocultural context in which shared meanings are exchanged and in which relationships are formed and explored, are less evident in current interpretations of curriculum and pedagogy, particularly in the UK.

A note about terminology

There are two terms on which this book centres that require clarification for the reader. The first of these is our use of the term 'role-play'. By role-play, we mean the 'shared pretend play between children in which they temporarily act out the part of someone else using pretend actions and utterances' (Harris, 2000: 30). In addition, we use the term role-play rather than fantasy, pretend or sociodramatic play as it was the term most readily used by the practitioners who participated in the study and referred to in the *Curriculum Guidance for the Foundation Stage* (QCA, 2000), the documentary guidance at that time for those working with children aged three to five in educational settings in England and Wales. The second term is 'reception class'. The reception class, a term with a particular currency in the UK, is the first class of primary school. It receives the new intake of children usually aged four or five. In England, Scotland and Wales, the statutory school starting age is the term after a child's fifth birthday. In practice, most children in England and Wales start school before the statutory age of five. In Chapter 1 we elaborate further on the background and context of the reception class. In addition, a glossary is available to explain other terms that are specific to the educational context in the UK.

Structure and content of book

Chapter 1 sets the scene for the educational provision of four-year-olds in the UK and presents a brief overview of how play in school has been located in wider discourses of developmental psychology and the traditions of early childhood education. Chapter 2 reviews some of the literature on role-play in early development in order to demonstrate its complexity and importance in the lives of children when they enter into school. Chapter 3 describes the research, design of the project and methodology, including the research process and some of the challenges we faced in researching young children's perspectives. Chapter 4 describes the classroom contexts and teachers' perspectives on role-play. Chapters 5 and 6 focus on role-play from the children's perspectives. In Chapter 5 we give the children's views on role-play, what they liked and didn't like and what was important to them. We also discuss the ways in which they challenge and resist adult authority in order to achieve their desired aims. Chapter 6 raises a number of tensions and dilemmas for children and practitioners around the issues of space, place and gender as they relate to role-play, while children's gendered play behaviours are discussed alongside pedagogical practices. Finally, in Chapter 7 we reflect on the project findings and suggest that these might make a modest contribution to debate about what constitutes a pedagogy of play in the UK and elsewhere.

Chapter 1

Four-year-olds in school
Play, policy and pedagogy

Introduction

A headline in a British national newspaper in 2005 announced 'Four-year-olds struggling with writing!' The article went on to explain:

> One in three young children are struggling to develop their early writing skills properly ... Statistics published by the Department for Education and Skills showed 32% of four-year-olds were not developing fast enough with the skill of linking sounds and letters.
>
> (Guardian Press Association, 2005, Thursday October 13)

To many of our international readers, such comments must seem extraordinary. At a time when most young children in Europe and elsewhere in the Western world are experiencing a kindergarten education based mainly on a diet of play and socialisation, many four-year-olds in England are apparently already failing to develop 'fast enough' in order to meet government targets. It is well known that the media are highly selective in what they report and how, and that there is a relationship between the media and the 'moral panics' that have punctuated policy debate throughout the history of education (Critcher in Buckingham, 2003). While we do not want to be unduly negative about the ways in which young children are portrayed in the media and elsewhere, the media nevertheless reflect cultural expectations as well as contributing to them. Moreover, it is certainly not our intention to promote a moral panic about the education of four-year-olds. Rather, our aim in this book is to contribute to the growing research literature that argues that there is a great deal more to the present and future lives of four-year-olds than whether or not they can link sounds and letters. So, while it might seem odd to begin a book about children's role-play with an explicit reference to government targets on writing, the wider context of early years education, in particular cultural and societal expectations of children's achievements reflected in the unusually early school starting age in the UK, provides the backdrop to the research reported in this book and to many of the arguments we put forward here.

We will argue that observing some of the ways in which children engage with role-play shows that, for them, school is about much more than targets for reading and writing. We learned also that by capitalising on some of the generic features of role-play – its transformative and aesthetic qualities (what Guss (2005) describes as 'dramatic intelligence') – we may be able to reconsider the extent to which it is positioned primarily as a tool for pedagogy, a vehicle for learning 'real-world things' (Strandell, 2000), and valued mainly for the ways in which it reproduces (rather than transforms) and rehearses the expectations of society (Guss, 2004). Later, in Chapter 2, we argue that 'being four' is a pivotal time in human development and that role-play is central to this. Of course, we are referring here to an imaginary, prototypical four-year-old, but nevertheless extensive research would seem to support the notion that between the ages of three and five children's play becomes especially rich, integrating a number of essential attributes that lay important foundations for later learning. If this is so, we might ask why, in England at least, we place so much emphasis on the importance of 'linking sounds and letters' and, moreover, introduce the notion of 'failure' into the discourse of education for children who are not yet of statutory school age.

Starting points for starting school

Educational provision for children under five in the UK is offered within a range of diverse settings in both the maintained and private sectors. Historically, the fragmented and patchy nature of this provision has created difficulties and divisions for children, their families and practitioners alike. Early childhood services in the UK have seen an unprecedented period of development and change since the election of the Labour government in 1997. The government's agenda to ameliorate the divisive and fragmented nature of early years provision in the UK is closely bound up with the desire to reduce child poverty and disadvantage and to encourage more lone parents (and in particular mothers) back to work. Such aspirations have required a major 'root and branch' approach to services for young children and their families (Anning, 2006). Central to this has been the dual aim both to increase the quantity and improve the quality of childcare provision.

This is not the place to describe in any real detail the complex and copious policies and initiatives that currently exist in the early years sector (for a comprehensive overview of policy, see Baldock et al., 2005); rather we want to set the scene for the four-year-olds in this research study. In 2000, a Foundation Stage for children aged three until the end of the reception year in school was established in England and Wales, supported by the *Curriculum Guidance for the Foundation Stage* (CGFS) (QCA, 2000). The aim of this initiative was twofold: first, to establish a long-awaited and distinct educational phase for young children, and second, to clarify for practitioners working with young children key areas of learning and appropriate progression towards Key Stage 1 of the National Curriculum. In broad terms this initiative was welcomed by early childhood practitioners since it provided a bridge between nursery and Key Stage 1, stressed flexibility and informality in the reception year, focused on child development, practical play and outdoor activity, and provided good guidance for teachers (adapted from Aubrey *et al.*, 2002). The CGFS also gives prominence to children's socio-affective, linguistic and imaginative development. Such radical changes to the curriculum, and the long-awaited recognition that the reception class was best seen as part of early years rather than of primary education, brought with it the promise of debate about raising the school starting age to six. However, despite major change and development across all areas of policy in the early years sector, one aspect that has remained remarkably resistant to change in the UK is the statutory school starting age.

In England, Wales and Scotland, the statutory school starting age is '5 and-a-bit' (Drummond, 2005: 83), described in official documentation as 'the term after a child's fifth birthday' (QCA, 2000). In Northern Ireland it is currently four, although following a recent major review of pre-school provision this is set to change to five. The decision to begin compulsory schooling at five in England was established as long ago as the Education Act of 1870. The basis for this decision had little to do with either developmental or educational criteria and was more closely related at that time to child protection issues on the one hand (children must be 'withdrawn from evil and corrupting influences' (cited in Read, 2006)), and an attempt to accommodate economic pressures on the other (an early starting age justified an early leaving age in order that children could join the workforce) (Woodhead, 1989). By way of contrast, the school leaving age in England has been raised incrementally on several occasions since compulsory schooling began: in 1918 it was raised to fourteen, in 1947 to fifteen, and in 1972 to sixteen.

Though the school starting age is set officially at five, in practice the majority of children in England enter the reception classes of primary schools at four. The latest figures available at the time of writing note that 62 per cent of four-year-olds are in reception classes of primary or infant schools (DfES, 2007). In the global context, the UK is certainly unusual in its policy of admitting children to school at age four or five rather than the more common European and international age of six and sometimes seven (Woodhead, 1989; Daniels *et al.*, 1995; Sharp, 2002; Gelder and Savage, 2004; Rogers and Rose, 2007).

Since its inception, concerns have been expressed about this unusually young school starting age, with policy reports and research studies having documented with great regularity over the decades unease both with the practice of admitting such young children into formal educational settings, and with the kinds of provision they encounter. To illustrate, consider the finding of the report of the Committee of Council on Education for the year 1897–98. Here the author writes: 'I fear that many years will elapse before little children under the age of six are delivered from the tyranny of books and slates' (in Read, 2006: 316). More than three decades later in 1931, the authors of the *Consultative Committee Report on the Primary School* noted 'a mistaken zeal for the initiation of children at too early an age to formal instruction' (in Read, 2006: 316). More recently still, David writes of 'the grave concern about the kinds of provision the majority of these four-year-olds, those in primary school reception classes, are experiencing' (1990: 5).

In spite of these concerns, there is little evidence of a serious challenge to the official school starting age or the practice of admitting four-year-olds to school, with one notable exception. It seems that proposals to raise the school starting age from five to six were discussed at some length in 1922 by the Committee on National Expenditure (personal correspondence with Kevin Brehony). This group of prudent businessmen estimated that such a move would produce a saving of some £1.7 million (Simon, 1991). The proposal was eventually rejected, and the trend to admit four-year-olds into reception classes in the year of their fifth birthday has continued to the present day (David, 1990; Taggart, 2004; Adams *et al.*, 2004). Now, as it was then, the practice is, arguably, more the outcome of economic and political expediency than well-considered educational aims (Gelder and Savage, 2004). As socio-economic conditions take precedence over debate and reasoning about what is best for children's learning (Rogers and Rose, 2007), Sharp concludes in an exhaustive review of literature relating to the school starting age that 'there is no compelling educational rationale for a statutory school age of five or for the practice of admitting four-year-olds to school reception classes' (2002: 20).

A recent increase in the number of young four-year-olds entering school may be due to a number of factors. First, falling school rolls create pressures for schools simply to fill places. Second, there may be pressure from parents for their children to start school earlier because of a lack of free pre-school provision, along with the perceived educational benefits of early admission to school. These factors may also contribute to successive governments' resistance to review school admissions policies (Daniels *et al.*, 1995 in Rogers and Rose, 2007; Baldock *et al.*, 2005). Third, the National Curriculum has exerted an indirect pressure within primary education to ensure that children have sufficient time in school before formal assessment at seven (Daniels *et al.*, 1995) so that teachers may feel under pressure to prioritise formal teaching in the areas of literacy and numeracy above a developmentally appropriate curriculum based on play, socialisation and talk (Adams *et al.*, 2004; Gelder and Savage, 2004; Fisher, 2000; Bennett *et al.*, 1997).

Reports on admission policies have raised important concerns about the quality of provision for these young four-year-olds in reception classes (e.g.

Rumbold Report, see DES, 1990; HMI Report 1988/9 cited in Cleave and Brown, 1991), noting in particular a lack of appropriately trained staff and restrictions on adequate space and resources. It is important to note that these reports have at the same time endorsed nursery-style provision for four-year-olds (Rogers and Rose, 2007). In 1995, 85 per cent of local authorities reported a single-point-of-entry policy, with only 15 per cent operating a mixed policy (Daniels *et al.*, 1995). In light of the variation and, some would say, discrepancies between admissions policies, it is not unreasonable to suggest that any policy decision ought to be based on whether or not this is beneficial for the children. A recent review of research on the advantages and disadvantages of single-point admission to school identified a number of key considerations if children in reception classes are to receive the high quality educational experiences to which they are entitled (as set out in the *Curriculum Guidance for the Foundation Stage* and the proposed Early Years Foundation Stage). These can be summarised as follows:

- There is a need for training for head teachers and non-early years specialist teachers in reception classes regarding appropriate curriculum, pedagogy and assessment for this age group.
- Some improvements in organisation and allocation of internal classroom space to encourage more active modes of learning and social interaction are likely to be needed too.
- Considerable effort will be needed to ensure universal outdoor provision for children in reception classes and where possible with free-flow access between indoor and outdoor areas.
- Increased and appropriate adult–child ratios may be needed in some settings.
- Less emphasis on preparation for Key Stage 1, formal, large group 'sit down' tasks is needed in reception classes in favour of a much greater emphasis on active, play-based learning, both indoors and outdoors. This is endorsed by Sanders *et al.* (2005) in research on transitions between reception and Key Stage 1.
- Young four-year-olds in school should receive an equal share of qualified teacher time so that they are not marginalised by the perceived 'academic' needs of older children in preparation for entry to Key Stage 1.
- Clear guidance for parents about what constitutes an appropriate curricular experience for children in the Foundation Stage, regardless of whether they are in the school context or elsewhere, is needed. This is imperative to counter increased and unrealistic expectations of children's academic achievement as a corollary to early entry to school.
- There is a need for greater awareness on the part of schools of the changing context in services for young children to avoid the gap which currently exists between 'pre-school' agencies in England and Wales such

as Sure Start and 'school' agencies such as the Qualifications and Curriculum Authority and the National Primary Strategy.

• Continuity, progression and integration of services for this age group, irrespective of where they are placed, are vital to the maintenance of quality provision in the early years.

(Rogers and Rose, 2007: 59–60)

Research into the educational benefits of an early school starting age suggests that the actual length of a child's education appears to matter less than the quality of the experience. Inappropriate provision may in fact be detrimental to children regardless of their starting age, and children who start formal schooling at a later age seem to outperform those who start earlier. The debate about the time at which a child starts school may, then, be less significant than the debate about the nature and quality of provision. If the provision is suitable to the developmental needs of young children, it appears that early attendance at school may be an advantage (as it is for pre-school attendance, see Sylva *et al.*, 2004). The challenge seems to lie, then, not in adopting a particular entry system, but in developing educational practices 'which better match the style of young children's learning in the early stages of acquisition' (Kavkler *et al.*, 2000: 84). Arguably, the most pressing need in the field of early childhood is to develop and implement a coherent and sufficiently responsive pedagogy for all children under five wherever they may be located.

In England and Wales, the legislated curriculum framework offers this possibility, endorsing a play-based, informal curriculum and pedagogy that is designed to be responsive to the developmental, social and physical needs of children in this age group. In turn this is informed by a robust research literature in which there is compelling evidence that children aged three to five are particularly receptive to peer group play activities that nurture imagination and creativity, and that develop social competence (Piaget, 1962; Sutton-Smith, 1971; Rubin, 1980; Smith, 1990, 2005; Corsaro, 1997; Trawick-Smith, 1998) and that such skills will ultimately support the development of literacy and numeracy, positive dispositions and well-being, thus laying firm foundations for lifelong learning (Laevers, 1993; Katz, 1999). This position is further strengthened by recent perspectives from neuroscience which argue that space, time and flexible open-ended resources appear to be significant in the healthy growth, well-being and intellectual development of young children (Bergstrom and Ikonen, 2005). However, less attention has been paid to precisely how a play-based curriculum might be implemented in classrooms of primary schools.

Interest in the state of children's play in school has, arguably, been eclipsed by the more serious, immediate and pressing concerns engendered by serial educational legislation and initiatives orientated around the concerns of primary schooling rather than early years provision. It was against this background that the present research developed.

A brief history of play in school

Play at the centre

That children 'learn through play' is a central and long-established tenet of the nursery and infant tradition which has shaped and continues to shape early childhood pedagogy as we know it to the present day. A central and defining feature of this tradition, well documented in the literature (see for example Bennett *et al.*, 1997), is the belief that play is necessary to healthy growth and development and is the natural and, therefore, most appropriate way in which young children learn (see for example Isaacs, 1933; Bruce, 1991; Beardsley and Harnett, 1998; Moyles, 2005). Play activity in early childhood education features also in a succession of government reports that have punctuated the debate to the present day and particularly since the publication of the Plowden Report (CACE, 1967) entitled *Children and their Primary Schools* (see for example DES, 1990; QCA, 2000; DfES, 2007).

A trawl of the vast literature on play in early childhood education returns a wide range of claims for its value and significance in young children's learning and development. Play scholars argue that children express their current interests and needs, and develop social and linguistic competence, through peer group play activity (Johnson, 1990; Corsaro, 1985), and that they exercise control over the environment, materials and outcomes, and acquire mastery of a range of skills, through the processes of imitation, exploration and practice (Piaget, 1962). Play can serve as a window on the child's developmental status, personality and well-being (Johnson, 1990; Pellegrini and Boyd, 1993). Moreover, it is argued that learning resides in the act of play itself, that it creates its own context for learning (Vygotsky, 1978; King, 1992), and that play is the child's work (Isaacs, 1929). Scholarly interest in the play of children is of relatively recent inception, traceable in part to the emergence of psychology as an autonomous discipline in the late nineteenth century. In carving out a space for itself within and between the existing disciplines of natural history, anthropology, physiology and medicine in particular (Burman, 1994), psychology conformed to a larger tendency of an age of science, of positivism and of incipient modernity. Both scientific modalities and the discourse of modernity promoted the measurement and classification of behaviours, abilities and dispositions in ways that were particularly apt for the study of children. In many ways this can be viewed as the late-nineteenth-century culmination of an Enlightenment project concerned with the increasing specialisation and progressive rationalisation of categories of knowledge. In a compelling deconstruction of the effects of developmental psychology in society at large, Burman notes the rise of child study 'societies' in the late nineteenth and twentieth centuries, their purpose to observe, weigh and measure children, 'documenting their interests, states and activities' (1994: 11). It is rather clear, then, that play provided an ideal site for the quasi-scientific observation of children's 'natural' interests, behaviours and mood states. Moreover, such observation, with its roots in the scientism and positivism of the late nineteenth century, continues to inform early childhood practice today. Since then, early childhood education has tended to align itself closely with the discipline of psychology, and in particular with studies of child development.

Another relevant pre-history of play in education lies in the Romantic movement, which took its definitive form in the imaginative culture of the late eighteenth century. The social theories of Jean-Jacques Rousseau were an important influence on this movement, and especially his idealisation of Nature and of 'natural man'. Rousseau's liberatory concerns were welded to a kind of nostalgia that was itself to become an important dimension of early Romanticism. The perceived dignity, spontaneity and expressiveness of the pre-civilised – whether of tribal peoples or of childhood innocence – represented conditions towards which man should aspire. In this sense the play of children, perfectly typified by the pupil Emile (in Rousseau's *Emile or On Education*), could be perceived as an exemplary model of ideal citizenry. From these intellectual roots, early education has evolved its own distinctive history grounded in a tradition whose ideas are deeply embedded in the ideological preoccupations of eighteenth- and nineteenth-century thinkers, and continued to resonate in the work of a succession of pioneer educators – Friederick Froebel, Maria Montessori, Susan Isaacs.

In more recent decades these ideas have come to be identified collectively as a 'child-centred' approach (Chung and Walsh, 2000), and aspects of this methodology have influenced profoundly the development of contemporary practice in both nursery and primary education. Indeed, it is difficult to separate the importance placed on children's play from the wider context of child-centred methodology. 'Learning through play' is frequently cited as a central component of the child-centred approach (Burman, 1994; Darling, 1994; King, 1992). Yet play at the same time embodies much of what we understand about the concept of child-centredness – its emphasis on active, experiential learning, the notion that children learn when they are 'ready', the emphasis on children's needs, and the importance of choice. Play, then, can also be viewed as the vehicle through which to express the core values of child-centred pedagogy. We can see how the 'play ethos' (Smith, 1988) stemming from this tradition over more than a century became the arena in which two fundamentally contrasting perspectives, namely a liberal-romantic philosophy of education, and an empirical-scientific approach, converged. Until the 1960s, there had been little empirical evidence to substantiate the view that play was essential to early learning. During the 1960s and 1970s, however, a growth in empirical research (which held real promise for proponents of play in education) resulted in a privileged period for studies of play, as intuitively based investigations of play were increasingly informed by scientific method. Such studies were in part fuelled by emergent child-centred ideas about education which were given their fullest expression at that time in the Plowden Report (CACE 1967) and by child-centred interpretations of Jean Piaget's theory of cognitive development, also popular at that time. Plowden gave public endorsement to belief in the inherent value of play in early learning ('play is the principal means of learning in early childhood' (1967: 193, para. 523)), and this endorsement, coupled with the rapid growth of research interest in play, enhanced greatly play's status in the classroom. In part, research also responded to methodologies developed within the larger fields of experimental psychology and biology. And interest at that time was directed not only towards understanding the role of play in human development *per se*, but also (and increasingly) with the possible cognitive and social benefits of play. The promise held out by scientifically conceived studies of play was, however, relatively short-lived (Smith, 1988). Subsequent analyses of several influential studies failed to replicate the positive findings that had linked play with learning, prompting Smith, a leading psychologist in the field, to write of a 'crisis' in play research (1988). As he saw it, this crisis was the result of inappropriate methodology but also of an inadequately developed theoretical framework. Indeed, Smith went on to call for a significant revaluation of the play ethos in early education. It would seem that in spite of widespread and sustained support for a play 'ethos' in early childhood education, there is surprisingly little evidence from empirical research to support the popular conception that play contributes substantially to young children's learning in school. In other words, there is a weighty theoretical literature on play regarding its ontological status and functional significance, but a relatively slender empirical literature examining specifically the relationships between play and learning, and between play and the contexts of schooling.

Play at the margins

In spite of the enduring centrality of play to early childhood education, expressed in the prevailing discourses of early childhood (Burman, 1994), a rather different picture of play is suggested in classroom-based research. During the 1980s a series of studies examined the nature and quality of education for the under-fives (Sylva *et al.*, 1980; Stevenson, 1987; Sestini, 1987; Hutt *et al.*, 1989; Bennett and Kell, 1989; Meadows and Cashdan, 1988) and was roundly critical of provision for play in both pre-school and statutory school settings. It was argued that in many activities observed in these studies children engaged in mainly stereotypical and repetitive behaviours with little evidence of cognitive challenge (Sylva *et al.*, 1980; Sestini, 1987; Hutt *et al.*, 1989). Later, Ofsted (1993) reported on the standards of education in reception classes and concluded that the quality of learning through play presented a rather 'dismal picture'. The report stated:

Fewer than half of the teachers observed fully exploited the educational potential of play. In more than a third of the schools visited, play was only recreational; it lacked educational purpose and was usually undertaken only after work had been completed.

(1993: 10)

Features of 'good practice' were also identified: careful planning, teacher involvement and the provision of activities with 'sound educational purpose'. The general focus of these criticisms is telling here. Note, for example, the emphasis throughout on 'purpose' and 'cognitive challenge' and the dismissal of play which is 'only recreational'. The insertion of the concept of 'play with a purpose' into the prevailing discourse of early childhood education, while not new, nevertheless gained greater and new significance in the post-ERA period. There is little trace of 'play with a purpose' in Plowden, save a reference to children's own purposes: 'The intense interest shown by young children in the world about them, their powers of concentration on whatever is occupying their attention or serving their immediate purposes, are apparent to both teachers and parents' (CACE, 1967: 195, para. 530). Compare with an extract from the so-called Rumbold Report, published in the wake of the studies of classroom practice noted above: 'For young children, purposeful play is an essential and rich part of the learning process' (DES, 1990: 7). We mention the issue of 'play with a purpose' here to illustrate a discernible shift in discourse pertaining to play that has taken place in recent years, gathering particular momentum during the 1990s, arguably reflecting the drive to make play more 'palatable' in school (Yardley in Atkin, 1991: 36) in relation to concomitant demands to deliver a subject-based curriculum. The discourse of 'play with a purpose' is most prevalent in reception classes, which are in turn located somewhat ambiguously in the borderlands between nursery education and statutory schooling. Nevertheless, recent studies of reception class practice note the continued divisions between play in thinking and play in practice (Bennett *et al.*, 1997; Adams, *et al.*, 2004; Aubrey, 2004), reflecting what Aubrey (2004) describes as competing discourses of school improvement versus a distinctive pedagogy for early childhood.

Play versus work

However we conceptualise play in early childhood education – as the free and expressive activity of the young, as a purposeful and instrumental activity, as a mechanism of cognitive development, or as a tool for learning in school (and these are not mutually exclusive categories) – the division between play and work is omnipresent. Conceptions of play are, of course, intimately tied to conceptions of childhood. Historians of childhood note how in the twentieth century there has been a progressive separation of childhood from adulthood:

'Children neither work nor play alongside adults; they do not participate in the adult world of law and politics' (Archard, 1993: 29). Within the modern conception of childhood our understanding of work and play is an index of this separation (Archard, 1993) and this constitutes the child as someone who plays; work is the polar opposite of play, and something only adults engage in. This is a peculiarly Western attitude; in non-Western societies the distinction between work and play seems rather less distinct. The imperative to play appears to be a universal characteristic of early childhood, but how play is understood within different societies and cultures in relation to other modes of activity varies significantly. Studies in the anthropology of play have found that the separation of work and play (i.e. labour and leisure) characteristic of industrialised societies is frequently absent in non-industrialised cultures, where more important contrasts are made between the sacred and the profane work or between play and ritual (Schwartzman, 1978). That is not to say that children living in the West today are not required to undertake work-like tasks in the home and school, and to assume progressively greater responsibility as they grow up; we might all remember undertaking such 'chores'. However, modern conceptions of childhood may not allow children *authentic* work experiences, since the real work of children is to play, as invoked in the epithet 'play is the child's work', which was first coined by Froebel and reconfigured by Isaacs half a century later: 'play is indeed the child's work and the means by which he grows and develops' (1929: 11). It is something of a paradox, then, that while there is an inherent separation between the activities of the child (play) and the activities of the adult (work), play cannot just be; it has to have a purpose (Cohen, 1993: 2). There is, of course, nothing new in this idea. Its origins can be traced to the earliest examples of play within pedagogical practice, in the Froebelian kindergarten, where play was used deliberately for educational ends (Cohen, 1993). Utilising play for educational purposes no doubt had considerable appeal in enlightened circles of nineteenth-century Europe. The philanthropic concern 'to release children from the bonds of work and confer the privileges of play' (Stone, 1971) coincided with the move to harness play for educational ends. In spite of these nineteenth-century roots, the institutionalisation of children's play is largely a twentieth-century phenomenon (Stone, 1971). But in the latter part of the twentieth century, 'play with a purpose' and the notion 'let's be serious about play' (Cohen, 1993) assumed an even greater significance in the rhetoric of educational policymakers. To illustrate this point in a more contemporary context, consider the language adopted in official documentation. For example, teachers are required to 'exploit' play's potential; play was 'only recreational and lacking in educational purpose' (Ofsted, 1993: 10). The provision of play activities with sound educational purpose is, then, the order of the day. This seems strangely at odds with the prevailing view, particularly where children are concerned (Cleave and Brown, 1991; Rogers and Evans, 2006), that play is by definition an intrinsically motivated and voluntary activity, free from adult-imposed demands. And can we infer from these comments that play without purpose (educational or otherwise) is viewed as a less worthwhile activity and a mere diversion (i.e. play cannot just be)?

Early childhood educators have long lamented the dichotomy between play and work that has pervaded Western discourse from the earliest pioneers (play is the child's work) to the present day. Play is inscribed in the literature as a voluntary (intrinsically motivated) activity in opposition to the obligatory nature of work. The division extends far beyond the immediate contexts of early education and its concomitant concerns with theories of learning, into the wider constellations of the historical and social divisions between work and leisure/recreation (Sutton-Smith and Kelly-Byrne, 1984). Perhaps this is why there is a tendency to idealise the child's play (Sutton-Smith and Kelly-Byrne, 1984), since it is already lost to us as we reach adulthood. It would seem that the division between play and work within the context of school is marked not simply by the ways in which play is often relegated to specific times and places, positioned in opposition to work, but also in the ways in which play, wherever it is enacted in school, is shaped by the contextual features that surround it.

Increasingly over recent decades, play in school has, arguably, taken on the characteristics and expectations of formal schooling, hijacked for the purposes of delivering a subject-based curriculum where the demand is to produce tangible outcomes and justifications for its place in the curriculum. Historically speaking, this came to a head in the years immediately following the introduction of the National Curriculum. Reflecting on this period, Pollard (1996) noted that the ideologies of 'New Right' politicians had consistently demonstrated a lack of appreciation of classroom conditions, of learning processes and of the motivational issues that are so important in work with young children. Although Pollard's work is concerned with the wider social context of young children's learning, his critique of the political and social context of education at that time is particularly apt in the study of play in school and the context of our research. The activity of play epitomises all that is child-centred in education. Its intrinsically motivated, spontaneous and voluntary characteristics are hardly compatible with the demands of an educational culture that prioritises accountability, measurable results and tangible outcomes. There has been a discernible shift in the discourse of play, and in the way in which we seek to understand its significance to young children in the context of pre-school or school. We should, perhaps, take note of Sutton-Smith's observation, made at the end of a long career in the field of play research: 'From Karl Groos ... to Piaget ... we have expected some payoff from play and have tried with great strenuousness to find it' (1995: 279). Perhaps, as Smith (1998) suggests, we should decouple the rather puritanical emphasis on the educational value of play from its more affective and life-enhancing qualities, remembering that Vygotsky, too, warned of a 'pedantic intellectualisation of play' (1978: 92).

While it is clearly difficult to demonstrate categorically that children learn through play in school, insights from developmental psychology demonstrate that play may serve a wide range of vital functions in human development and experience and that this may include learning in its broadest sense. As we have seen already, play provides the means by which children may encounter, assimilate and re-create newly acquired concepts and experiences. In this way play or perhaps 'playfulness' can be regarded as a methodology, an approach to education and learning, rather than a prescription for some tangible learning, and primarily cognitive, outcome. Yet we are still left with the problem of how to justify the place of play in school. After all, should we not expect play in school to serve a different purpose from play elsewhere? This is Moyles's view: 'Parents have a right to expect that play in school should be significantly and differently organised from play at home and elsewhere' (1989: 17). The distinction between play as such and play in school (Guha, 1988) is made by several writers. Hartup et al. (1993) distinguish between open-field and closed-field play, the former taking place spontaneously outside the school context, the latter within the socially confined and controlled space of the classroom. Here the juxtaposition of the spontaneous and controlled highlights the way in which play in school is never simply the 'free and spontaneous expression of childhood' (King, 1992). This is particularly true of children's play in reception classes.

Play and pedagogy

In many ways the coupling of play with pedagogy is problematic, not least because traditionally, the concept of play has been positioned in opposition to its more worthwhile counterpart, work, in the ways outlined above. This division is marked not simply by the ways in which play is often relegated to specific times and places, positioned in opposition to work, but also in the ways in which play, wherever it is enacted in school, is shaped by the contextual features that surround it. In earlier work on the relationship between play in theory and play in practice, Rogers (2000) argued that the pedagogy of play in school is characterised by complexity and diversity of practice, that it can be understood as the locus of interactions between the needs of the children and the needs of the teacher, between ideological and pragmatic imperatives, between spontaneous and intrinsically motivated actions of the child and the demands of a standardised and politicised curriculum, noting also that definitions of play pedagogy are defined principally from the adults' perspective without reference to how children respond to and make sense of pedagogical practices. In addition, play is widely regarded as a child-initiated activity, free from externally imposed rules, whereas pedagogy is viewed principally from the perspective of adults working in early childhood settings. Not surprisingly, then, agreement about what constitutes an appropriate pedagogy of play in early childhood education is hard to find. Wood has recently described a pedagogy of play as 'the ways in which early childhood professionals make provision for playful and play-based activities, how they design play/learning environments, and all the pedagogical techniques and strategies they use to support or enhance learning through play' (2005: 19). A useful distinction is also drawn in definitions of effective pedagogy between *pedagogical interactions* (specific behaviours on the part of adults) and *pedagogical framing* (the behind-the-scenes aspects of pedagogy which include planning, resources and establishment of routines) (Siraj-Blatchford and Sylva, 2004). However, within this model there is little reference to the children's part in shaping pedagogy, how they respond to certain pedagogical interactions, and to aspects of pedagogical framing. Devine notes that pedagogy is concerned with how learning takes place and is implicitly tied up with the exercise of power between teachers and pupils – between adults and children – framing children's learning in terms of certain goals and values (Devine, 2003: 53). Brooker's (2002) study of identity in children starting school demonstrates persuasively that pedagogy needs to be tuned in to children's cultural values which may not reflect the dominant values in the classroom. Pedagogy is, of course, also bound up with the larger contexts and agendas of education, with the practical exigencies of classroom life: in other words, with the realities of teachers and children 'living together' in schools (McLean, 1991). Certainly this is how we view the project classrooms and the day-to-day realities of the children and adults. Moreover, classrooms can be viewed as places of tension, struggle and dilemmas (Sugrue, 1997; Woods *et al.*, 1999), not simply as places where curriculum guidelines, educational theory, beliefs and ideals are put neatly into practice.

It is acknowledged widely in the literature from a sociocultural perspective that effective learning takes place within 'learning communities' where participants co-construct learning encounters through a process of reciprocal exchanges of meaning. These include studies of effective learning in schools (Carnell and Lodge, 2002) and practitioners developing practice together (Anning, 2004). In early childhood settings, an effective and appropriate curriculum is co-constructed between adults and more knowledgeable others (peers and adults) (Siraj-Blatchford and Sylva, 2004; Jordan, 2004: Wood, 2005) where both children and their educators are involved and where the content is in some way instructive (Siraj-Blatchford and Sylva, 2004: 720). The emphasis so far has been on co-constructing teaching and learning outcomes and curriculum. Yet growing support from sociocultural perspectives for children's agency and active involvement in shaping their environments suggests that a co-constructive relationship might also be applied more widely to pedagogy in early childhood settings.

Being four in school

Within the reception class as it is currently conceived, it would seem that the contribution of play to early learning continues to be highly variable and dependent on a range of external political, structural and managerial factors. In spite of significant improvements in some quarters in the early years sector, not least the capital investment in young children and their families, Anning argues that the 'historical baggage' such as low status and lack of training was carried forward into the new era (2006: 57). One further aspect of this baggage is, arguably, the apparent failure of policy-makers to grasp the very real differences that continue to exist between nursery and reception classes in terms of the implementation of a curriculum framework that is designed precisely to ensure parity and continuity between settings (Adams *et al.*, 2004). Against the background of continued criticisms of practice in reception classes it may be time to reconsider how they are organised and how learning opportunities are presented. Given the prevalence of young four-year-olds in these settings it seems even more pressing to develop pedagogy that reflects its position as the second year of the foundation stage, as part of early years, rather than simply as a preparatory stage to formal primary schooling. A number of recent policy and research initiatives, such as *Excellence and Enjoyment Strategy for Primary Schools* (DfES, 2003), proposals for a renewed emphasis on teaching creatively in schools (Craft, 2005), a recent government commissioned report entitled *Nurturing Creativity in Young People* (Roberts, 2006), the findings of Sylva *et al.* (2004) regarding pre-school education, and a recent report by Sanders *et al.* (2005) on transition from reception to Key Stage 1, endorse a rich and exciting experience at all levels of education through a wide range of learning strategies and flexible teaching and learning environments – a bottom-up rather than top-down model, particularly in reception and Year 1.

It is unlikely in the near future that the school starting age in England will be raised to six or seven. Nor is it economically and demographically possible or palatable to government for an expansion of nursery provision universally to accommodate children under five (Rogers and Rose, 2007). Therefore, any current and future debate about the school starting age is likely to centre on the question of the nature and quality of educational provision for children in the Foundation Stage in which play is clearly implicated. As we write, the imperative to resolve some of the tensions and dilemmas mentioned in this chapter is even more pressing as we contemplate the introduction of a new curriculum framework for children from birth to five in England and Wales (DfES, 2007).

For at least a decade it has been argued by early years experts that the reception class is a 'muddle in the middle' (Gelder and Savage, 2004). With young children described and perceived variously as 'rising fives' and as 'pre-school', it seems reasonable to ask the rhetorical question 'when is it OK to be four?' Moreover, recent global moves to consult young children about their educational and care experiences encourage practitioners, researchers and policy-makers alike to consider settings from the child's perspective (see for example Clark and Moss, 2001; Keating *et al.*, 2002). Taking all of these points into account, it is clear that ensuring appropriate provision must be the prerequisite of placing four-year-olds in reception classes. And this must include a consideration of the relationship between children's play and pedagogy. However, classroom-based evidence suggests that the nature of teaching and learning and its relationship to play has not yet been adequately theorised or conceptualised in ways that determine the most appropriate provision for children aged four and five in school. In light of this, our overarching question in this book is *what does play mean to children and teachers in reception classes?* A second, related question is: *how does play in school change play as such?* This is a vexed question. Should we expect play in school to embody the qualities of play as such? If not, is it 'play' of which we speak or some other activity constructed, modified and transformed by the contexts of schooling? It is also possible to argue that educational provision for children under five in school in the UK is still subject to a long history of political ambivalence, some would say expediency. While there have been unprecedented developments in the pre-school sector since 1997 in the UK, the policy of admitting children who are under five to reception classes in primary schools has remained unchanged and largely unchallenged. As we will argue throughout this book, play, and especially role-play, occupies a central place in this debate.

Chapter 2

Perspectives on role-play in early childhood

'Sssh the lion's asleep.' Jessica, aged four, took my hand as I entered her classroom for the first time, and led me on tiptoe towards the corner of the classroom where there was a 'cave' made out of cardboard, paper and paint. Inside the cave was a large toy lion, 'sleeping'. We sat together quietly in the cave for several minutes, until Jessica turned to me and said with some urgency, 'He's waking up now ... let's go'. This momentary suspension of reality required that, for a short time, both Jessica and I stepped out of the classroom and into a shared imaginary world.

(Field notes)

Introduction

We begin this chapter with an extract from some field notes made just before the start of the project. Several questions arose for us from this brief episode of shared pretence. First, *what capacities and skills has Jessica acquired in her four years to enable her to pretend in this way?* Second, *what are the benefits, if any, of this kind of play to current and later learning?* Finally, *what kind of pedagogy enables Jessica to initiate such imaginary encounters?* Taking this example as our starting point, in this chapter we present some perspectives from both theoretical and empirical research that may help us to address these questions and to unravel some of the complexities of role-play and its potential as a vehicle for learning in early schooling. Research from a range of disciplines and theoretical perspectives concludes that role-play is the predominantly preferred activity of social engagement in young children (Corsaro, 1997; Meckley, 1996), and that it provides an ideal context in which children can develop social competence (Rubin, 1980; Sutton-Smith, 1971) and a sense of well-being (Rubin, 1980), providing opportunities for the resolution of conflict (both social and cognitive) in authentic contexts (Piaget, 1962; Sutton-Smith, 1977; Trawick-Smith, 1998). Other studies argue that in role-play children both exhibit and extend their linguistic capabilities (Andreson, 2005; Bergen, 2002) and that children 'actively communicate and interpret their individual and collective social realities through the play frame'

(Meckley, 1996: 295). Thus role-play is a collective and inter-subjective experience and can help children both to develop insights into the perspectives of others and to confirm or challenge their own perspective on phenomena: 'the ability to imagine themselves taking a position that is different from their own' (Carpendale and Lewis, 2006: 39). Such are the claims for role-play in early childhood, that even a cursory glance at the burgeoning literature on the subject would seem to suggest that role-play or shared pretence activity is vitally important to children of pre-school age.

A great deal of what we know and understand about role-play stems from psycho-biological and cognitive-developmental perspectives, offering accounts of play that for some may seem too focused on individual experience and thus essentialise both children and childhood. Such perspectives have provided important insights into some of the innately patterned behavioural and psychological characteristics of play in human development and evolution, but they can in themselves tell us little about how, and in what ways specifically, the contexts of schooling shape and ultimately determine the course of children's play experiences (King, 1992: 58). More recently, it has become common in the early childhood literature to recognise the hegemony of de-contextualised approaches in the study of young children and the tendency of these approaches towards reductionism, and the fact that they point to a failure to recognise social and cultural diversity in the lives of young children and their families. Walsh, for example, has written recently about an over-reliance on developmental theory as the guiding force for early childhood pedagogy. At the same time, however, he alerts us to the dangers of simply replacing one narrow orthodoxy with another (Walsh, 2005: 46), suggesting instead that we look towards a contemporary developmental theory that recognises how the child is located within culture: 'culture is both the context *within* which the child develops and the context *into* which the child develops' (2005: 45, original emphasis). Clearly the suggestion is not to abandon altogether the important insights that developmental theory and research have cast on young children's thinking and learning. Rather we need to ensure that such insights are grounded in a more 'fully social' (Quicke, 1994) and cultural analysis of children's experiences. From a sociocultural standpoint we view children's role-play as incorporating agency on the part of the children. Sociocultural perspectives emphasise the role of social interaction in the transformation of interpersonal to intrapersonal functioning (Vygotsky, 1978; Wertsch, 1985). Learning is, therefore, a result of the individual's active participation and involvement in situated social practices, and not simply the result of knowledge transmission. From this perspective, socially interactive ways of working are viewed as creating highly effective learning situations. Therefore, the social construction of knowledge takes place through joint activity where children are guided by adults or more competent peers (Rogoff, 1990).

In the discussion that follows we are necessarily selective, highlighting first the ways in which the foundations of role-play are laid down in the early social interactions between young infants and the significant people around them. We also consider in more detail some of the dominant perspectives on role-play presented to us in the work of Piaget, Vygotsky and Smilansky. Each of these has in some seminal way contributed to our understanding of the relevance of play to early learning and education.

In the beginning

However we may describe it, as symbolic, fantasy, pretend, or role-play, the ability to move beyond the here and now, between belief and make-believe, is a profound and uniquely human achievement (White, 2002). To elaborate this point further, role-play has a special significance in human development for the ways in which it separates the play of children from the play of young animals. But as far as we know we are not born with this ability, only the potential for it. While practice or preparation play is associated with the 'lower functions' of play observed in young animals (Bailey and Farrow, 1998) (and the human capacity for reflection, language and concept formation does not preclude the presence of such basic traits), human play has the potential to go beyond the play of animals, as witnessed daily in the imaginative constructions of children's fantasy role-play and language play. For example, Finlay says, 'We're running out of petrol' and pretends to fill up the spaceship with petrol from the plastic tube as you would from a petrol pump at a garage, making pump noises as he does it. Steven announces in the café, 'I'm the police' (still wearing his chef's hat and pointing a salt pot like a gun), 'I'm a policeman not a chef and this is my gun'. Spacegirl exclaims from the spaceship, 'I've seen a rocket on the computer we're going to hit it' (blowing through plastic tube) 'ring, ring ... speak in to it' (giving other end of pipe to spaceman) 'we're going to crash'. These children, all between the ages of four and five, have already become highly skilled and competent players, distinguishing between what is real and what is not real, communicating intentions to another person while beginning to appreciate that they too will understand the game, and transforming real meaning (for example, the salt pot) into play meaning (the gun) (Andreson, 2005). Through role-play, notions of reality and fantasy can operate simultaneously. In addition, children must at any one moment in time engage with play partners, play props, and physical and temporal factors such as space, place and time. Moreover, the necessity to communicate, both verbally and non-verbally, both intra- and interpersonally, is overriding in role-play. In this sense we might describe role-play as encompassing a communication imperative. Role-play also involves, crucially, the ability to see and appreciate another viewpoint. But how and when do children acquire this enormously complex web of skills?

Clearly the social context into which children are born is highly significant in how and in what ways they acquire and utilise these skills. Moreover, how a culture values and therefore nurtures the emergent capacities of babies and infants will also vary and therefore shape the way in which these ultimately develop. In spite of cultural difference there seem to be a number of traits that are discernible across populations of children, that contribute to the young child's search for meaning and enable effective and satisfying social interaction. Pretend play, or role-play as we call it, appears to function as an important mechanism in both integrating many developmental traits and at the same time supporting the development of them, namely mental representation, theory of mind, the ability to communicate, and language acquisition.

Infants in the first year of life do not, as far as we are able to tell, engage in pretend play (Gopnik *et al.*, 1999; Harris, 2000; Piaget, 1962). Then, in the second year of life we see the emergence of pretence, and as it develops over the next few years so it becomes increasingly elaborate and varied. The roots of role-play can be traced to the early mental representations formed by young infants, a process that begins at birth. Object permanence in infants is often identified as the first obvious or testable evidence of children's ability to retain images or representations mentally (Baillargeon, 1987; Gopnik *et al.*, 1999), typically between six and nine months. Put simply, infants begin to 'hold' images of objects and people in their heads, even in their absence. Imagine if we couldn't do this; of course, you couldn't imagine at all without this powerful capacity for mental representation. It is beyond the scope and purpose of this chapter to discuss this particular cognitive milestone in any detail. Numerous experiments have sought to establish the point at which infants are able to remember rather than simply to recognise. Clearly this capacity is present very early in the first few months of life. But to use those representations deliberately as in pretence appears not to be evident until well into the second year. At this point we observe children engaging in simple imitative play with some symbolic activity, such as using a banana as a telephone. To do this, however, the child needs to have some understanding of two worlds – the world in which the banana is just a banana, and the world in which the banana can also become a telephone. It stands to reason that one needs to be able to retain and recall images of things and people experienced in order to enact them. But this is not the whole story. Genuinely shared pretence, which typically appears in children at about three years of age, also requires sophisticated social understanding. An important capacity that develops at around this time thus enables children to move beyond the early mental representations and symbolic activity observed in very young infants to increasingly complex, cooperative play. This is the development of a 'theory of mind', a term used widely in the literature (Wellman, 1990) to refer to children's emergent mind-reading ability, which develops gradually between the ages of two and six (Jenkins and Astington, 2000). This 'ability to infer mental states in ourselves and others' (Bailey, 2002: 163) is an essential human life skill, marking an important milestone in children's development (Dunn, 2004), and underpinning the beginning of empathy, aptly described by Baron-Cohen as a 'leap of imagination into someone else's head' (2003: 26). Hobson notes that 'one needs experience of other people (with minds) in order to acquire concepts of mind in the first place' (2002: 242). Social inter-action and social referencing, that is reading the outward signs of others' reactions and behaviours, are vital in this process. The youngest babies soon learn how to react to the outward signs of other minds before they are fully aware that they exist (Gopnik *et al.*, 1999). This ability appears typically in children around the ages of three and four, just at a point where there is a sig-nificant increase in the incidence of shared pretend play. So does pretend play help in the development of a theory of mind or is it the product of it? It appears that the jury is still out on this matter, although Dunn (2004) sug-gests that children's pretend play, especially *shared* pretence (our emphasis), may be particularly significant for the development of theory of mind, and it is likely that there is a reciprocal relationship between them.

Alternative realities: the importance of being four

For many three- and four-year-olds entering the social world of early child-hood settings for the first time, role-play is fast becoming a highly complex social activity in which a network of skills is already becoming established. In order for children to demonstrate competence and complexity in early childhood settings, pedagogy needs to accommodate cultural and linguistic diversity. According to several research studies the ability to 'mind-read' is considerably more advanced in four-year-olds than in many three-year-olds (Gopnik *et al.*, 1999). At around the age of four, children also demonstrate an increasingly secure appreciation that 'our minds are not simply a copy of reality' (Carpendale and Lewis, 2006: 36). Dunn notes that at between three and four years of age the ability to take on complementary roles within a rule-governed context increases rapidly (2004: 31). So perhaps it is no coin-cidence that children in their fourth and fifth year are especially preoccupied with shared pretence.

Jessica is typical here, in that she spent a great deal of her free time in school during her fifth year creating shared imaginary worlds with her peers. If we revisit Jessica's episode of pretence at the beginning of this chapter, we can see that she is evidently aware of two realities (what is real and what is not real) and, even more impressive, she communicates this to another person subtly through the invitation to play: 'Sssh, the lion's asleep'. Jessica is delib-erately creating an alternative reality, exemplifying Hobson's point that 'one cannot accidentally pretend', indeed, that the very point of pretending is the fact that 'one chooses to make this stand for that' (2002: 78). It is precisely this intentional juxtaposition of two realities that defines role-play, relying as it does upon this awareness on the part of the player of alternative possible worlds, of two sets of goals and rules, 'one operating here and now, one that applies outside the given activity' (Csikszentmihalyi, 1981). We should be clear, however, that reality is not some fixed, permanent state, but is relative: contingent and constructed relative to the goals that cultures and individuals create: 'for each person, reality is defined in terms of the goals he or she invests attention in at any one time' (1981: 17).

The point has already been made that there is an imperative to communicate in role-play, whether directly through verbal forms of language or through more subtle repertoires of play signals, which may include facial expression, gesture and symbolic transformations. In studies of rough and tumble play, Smith (2005) describes how children adopt 'play faces' to distinguish between real fighting and play fighting, and that by the time they are four, children are able both to recognise and explain these and other cues present in play (2005: 132). A defining feature of role-play is what Bateson (1973) describes as meta-communication. By this he means the forms of communication used by children to define the boundaries between behaviour that is 'inside' the role-play and that which lies outside it. According to Andreson (2005), metacommunication may serve several important functions within the play:

- it lays out the boundaries between play and reality;
- it transforms meanings of things, persons, actions and context;
- it enables children to plan the next steps of the plot by leaving the play and then speaking about what to do next.

(adapted from Andreson, 2005: 390)

An example will help to illustrate this in action. Roxanne and Mia are playing in 'the café'. Roxanne says to Mia, 'You can pretend to take an order but you're not the baby'. Roxanne runs out of the café and says, 'Can I have a piece of paper please to go in the café?' Roxanne returns with the paper and says to Sally in a 'grown-up' voice, 'Right, what would you like madam?' When Roxanne says to Mia, 'You can pretend to take an order' she is using meta-communication about play in order to plan for and organise the play.

Distinguishing play from learning: re-reading Piaget

Piaget wrote extensively on the subject of play, yet it is interpretations of his theories about the nature of intelligence that have had most influence within early childhood pedagogy. Piaget's work represents a shift away from the environmental behaviourism (note the well known metaphor depicting children as 'empty vessels') prevalent in the early part of the twentieth century, towards a model of development that was interactionist in orientation. In so doing, Piaget invoked an alternative metaphor. The child, no longer an 'empty vessel', became the 'architect' of her/his own learning, actively constructing knowledge from her/his interactions with the world. It was this single idea in particular that attained such immense popularity in education (Burman, 1994; Sutherland, 1994). Essential to an understanding of Piaget's work is the notion that the nature of children's thought is qualitatively different at each stage of development, and that we learn by a process of adjustment to the environment. Intelligence can thus be defined in an evolutionary sense as adaptation. For Piaget, two mechanisms inform the learning process. The first of these, *accommodation*, requires that the child adapt (change) to fit the demands of the environment. In contrast, the second mechanism, *assimilation*, requires that the child adapt (change) the environment to suit his/her imagination.

Piaget regards play as mainly an assimilative activity and thus not directly correlated with learning as he defines it within his broader theoretical framework: 'Play is primarily mere functional or reproductive assimilation' (1962: 87). Through the assimilative process the function of play is essentially to incorporate old skills into new ones as the child adjusts the environment to suit his/her desires and needs. Adjustment can take place through practice and repetition, whereby the child can modify and vary behaviours and gestures associated with the original newly learned act. Thus we see a separation of the essential core of a skill from the inessential elaborative variations that are typical of play. This is why play may at times appear unfocused and spontaneous, and can incorporate a variety of seemingly unrelated movements and gestures (Rubin *et al.*, 1983). Rather than view play as mere reproduction, we might think of the assimilative activity of pretend play as an 'elaboration on a learned theme', as an imaginative construction, whose formation gives a creative complexion to even the most mundane aspects of imitation and repetition associated with the activity. It follows logically that in making the novel familiar, greater understanding accrues: 'to invent is to understand' (Piaget, 1962).

Through the mechanism of assimilation, Piaget argues, children incorporate events, objects or situations into existing ways of thinking. Play represents an imbalance or *disequilibrium* in which assimilation dominates accommodation. If every act of intelligence is equilibrium between assimilation and accommodation, while imitation is a continuation of accommodation for its own sake, it may be said conversely that play is essentially assimilation or the primacy of assimilation over accommodation (Piaget, 1962: 87). In turn, the behaviour resulting from this assimilative orientation reflects the child's level of development. The pleasure (or affective value) of practice play comes from the child's sense of control over self and the environment, or 'functional pleasure' as Piaget termed it (ibid.). Put simply, Piaget's central point is that initial learning is adaptation, but that the subsequent repetition and variation, once consolidated, is play.

For children passing through Piaget's preoperational stage (age two to six years), symbolic play is, he argues, the dominant mode and reflects the appearance and development of the basic semiotic function, that one thing (the signifier) stands for another (the signified) (Rubin *et al.*, 1983). Piaget is clear that symbolic play is still an assimilative act. But there is a profound shift from actions exercised and elaborated for their functional value (as observed in infants passing through the sensorimotor stage) to actions exercised for their representational value. For example, Jake picks up the 'pepper pot' to use as the baby's bottle and says, 'I'm going to take the milk and you're never having this back!' The symbols of pretence also come from deferred imitations of others (Piaget, 1962). These observed and reproduced behaviours may not reflect the child's direct experience, but in play they are given meaning that fits the child's current understanding.

Piaget's location of play at the assimilative end of the learning spectrum may appear to devalue its functional role in cognition. For Harris (2000), Piaget's analysis of pretend play is a negative one in that it is presented as an activity that gives way to more logical ways of thinking and behaving. In other words, children grow out of it as they become more rational. Furthermore, Piaget fails to acknowledge several important features evident in joint pretence, such as drama and fiction, and, importantly, representations rather than reproductions of reality (Harris, 2000: 24). Harris explains that Piaget 'conflates two different issues, the inspiration for and act of pretence and what it is meant to signify' (ibid.). Similarly, Sutton-Smith's main criticism of Piaget's view of play 'as a transient, infantile stage in the emergence of thought' (1971: 334) is that it is too narrow an interpretation of the phenomenon, negating the many and varied forms of play, ultimately undermining its significance in human experience. He offers instead a broader, more holistic conception of human adaptation in relation to play:

> Play is not solely a cognitive function (nor solely affective or conative), but an expressive form *sui generis* with its own unique purpose on the human scene. It does not subserve 'adapative' thought as Piaget defines it (though of course it can do that); it serves to express personal meanings.
>
> (1971: 341)

It is often noted that Piaget's work contains a caveat in terms of the importance of the social context and the significance of others in the development and learning of young children. However, this tends to eclipse discussions of the importance Piaget placed on the impact of peer relations as providing the means by which children resolve cognitive conflict (disequilibrium) in the context of conflict (social and/or intellectual) between peers. Children are less likely explicitly to challenge the wisdom and authority of an adult due to unequal power relations. In this sense, Piaget offers early childhood educators a compelling rationale for providing children with ample opportunities for peer group role-play (see also Siraj-Blatchford *et al.*, 2004). We can also attribute to Piaget our appreciation of the differences in the ways children and adults think (Baldock, 2006).

Piaget's work relating to early childhood is not short of critics. In particular there has been a focus on the way in which Piaget's model is 'unable to theorise cultural and historical change in relation to the development of knowledge' (Burman, 1994: 154) together with an emphasis on his depiction of the child 'who is irrevocably isolated and positioned outside history and society' (ibid.). Critics have also argued that Piaget's work positioned the teacher at the margins of children's learning, and indeed play (Walkerdine, 1986; Meadows and Cashdan, 1988), and promulgated a *laissez-faire* approach to teaching and learning for young children (Meadows and Cashdan, 1988; Wood and Attfield, 2005). Of course, this latter point was not Piaget's intention but a result of subsequent interpretations of his theories in practice. It is not our purpose here to defend criticisms of Piaget's ideas, nor can we do justice either to Piaget's original thesis on play or to subsequent interpretations of his works: these are both extensive and complex. Whatever one's view on Piaget, it is difficult to ignore his importance in shaping all our thinking about education. At the same time it is rather too easy to reject out of hand the important insights he has offered into the structures of cognition and play.

Vygotsky: play, imagination and rules

Definitions of play and role-play proliferate in the literature. A particularly useful definition is that proposed by Vygotsky, whose work has become well known in recent decades. Role-play is regarded as especially significant in the work of Vygotsky, for whom 'play' meant 'role-play' (Hannikainen, 1995). Vygotsky (1978) emphasised in particular the significance of imagination, internal rules and the presence of role in the characterisation of play. Vygotsky's output, located as it is within wider currents of sociocultural models of development, has gained considerable currency in recent decades and his work is now widely documented and discussed in the educational literature (for example, Wood and Wood, 1996; Pollard, 1993, 1996; Daniels, 1993; Wertsch, 1985). Sociocultural perspectives emphasise the role of social interaction in the transformation of interpersonal to intrapersonal functioning (Vygotsky, 1978; Wertsch, 1985). Learning is, therefore, a result of the individual's active participation and involvement in situated social practices, and not simply the result of knowledge transmission. From this perspective, socially interactive ways of working are viewed as creating highly effective learning situations. Therefore, the social construction of knowledge takes place through joint activity where children are guided by adults or more competent peers (Rogoff, 1990). These ideas are contained within what is, arguably, Vygotsky's most immediately accessible and useful concept for educators, the so-called *zone of proximal development* (ZPD). Its significance is so widely documented that it is unnecessary to provide a detailed discussion of its nature here. However, a brief description may be useful. Vygotsky described the ZPD as the 'distance between the actual developmental level as determined by independent problem-solving and the level of potential development as determined through problem solving under adult guidance or in collaboration with more capable peers' (1978: 86). Thus the social (interpersonal) becomes the individual (intrapersonal). These in turn are mediated by tools – the disciplines and practices – created by the culture. According to Vygotsky, 'Every function in the child's cultural development appears twice: first, on the social level, and later, on the individual level; first, between people (interpsychological), and then inside the child (intrapsychological)' (1978: 57).

From a sociocultural perspective the development of mind is related both to biological development and to the appropriation of cultural heritage (Wertsch, 1985; Cole, 1996); thus the nature of the individual's activity and cognitive development cannot easily be isolated from its social, historical and cultural context. But how does this relate to children's play? Vygotsky wrote very little about play specifically, but his consideration of play, contained in one brief chapter in a collection of papers entitled *Mind in Society*, belatedly published in 1978, is profoundly insightful, and to this day offers a uniquely formulated exposition of the function of play in development. Vygotsky accorded play a position of critical importance in his general theory of development (Newman and Holzman, 1993). Thus Vygotsky states that 'play is not the predominant feature of childhood but it is a leading factor in development' (1978: 101). Yet, perhaps ironically, it is not Vygotsky's theory of play that has been applied widely to discussions of play in early childhood education, but his more general theories of development and instruction. Indeed, Newman and Holzman make a similar point, noting the paucity of Vygotsky-inspired research on play (1993: 94). Of particular interest to our understanding of role-play is the way in which Vygotsky defines play. His central point is that the 'imaginary situation' is characteristic of all play and not simply of what we refer to as role-play or fantasy-play activity. Indeed, as he explains, this is what distinguishes play from other kinds of activity:

> in establishing criteria for distinguishing a child's play from other forms of activity, we conclude that in play a child creates an imaginary situation. This is not a new idea, in the sense that imaginary situations in play have always been recognised; but they were previously regarded as only one example of play activities. The imaginary situation was not considered as the defining characteristic of play in general but was treated as an attribute of specific subcategories of play.
>
> (1978: 934)

A second defining characteristic, and one that is linked inextricably with the creation of an imaginary situation, is the presence of rules: 'whenever there is an imaginary situation in play, there are rules – not rules that are formulated in advance and change during the course of the game but ones that stem from an imaginary situation' (1978: 95). He gives the example of a child playing the role of mother. The child, he argues, is bound by the rules of what it means to be a mother, not purely in the sense of a particular mother, but rather within the rules of 'maternal behaviour' (ibid.). At the same time, Vygotsky argues, when children engage in games with rules (and here he gives the example of chess), they are still enacted within an imaginary situation. Thus he concludes that 'just as we are able to show ... that every imaginary situation contains rules in a concealed form, [so] the reverse – that every game with rules contains an imaginary situation in a concealed form' (ibid. 95–96). In terms of children's development, the transition from play, in which rules are subservient to imagination, to games, in which the imagination is subservient to rules, outlines the evolution of children's play (ibid.). Vygotsky's discussion of play includes also a consideration of the relationship between meaning (thought) and action. In play, he argues, thought is separated from objects, and action arises from ideas rather than things; a piece of wood begins to be a doll and a stick becomes a horse (ibid. 96). He explains that in the very young child, action on objects is dominant over meaning. However, an important developmental shift takes place as the child begins to engage in symbolic activity. This is play rather than pure imitation (cf. Piaget), characterised by the subordination of action to meaning.

For Vygotsky, the play–development relationship can be compared to the instruction–development relationship. But he suggests that 'play provides a much wider background for changes in needs and consciousness' than is possible in instruction as he conceives it between the child and the more knowledgeable other. The central point for early childhood educators is that play creates its own ZPD, in which the child moves forward and which makes play the 'highest level of pre-school development' (Vygotsky, 1978: 103). Play, then, is of central importance to the young child's development, not least because it 'continually creates demands on the child to act against immediate impulse' (1978: 99). The child at play is bound by the rules of the game (whether playing 'mother' or chess); he/she is positioned in a force-field between his/her desire to act spontaneously and by the inherent need to subordinate those desires to the rules of the game. Thus Vygotsky contends that 'the child's greatest control occurs in play' (ibid.). This is of profound importance in our understanding of role-play's contribution to children's development. There is no mention of curriculum subjects or academic achievement as such. Rather the real benefit of play is that it enables young children to demonstrate, practise and simply experience self-control. The rule-bound nature of play, the self-control children require in play in order that the play is sustained, emphasises the importance of play between children whether or not they are more or less knowledgeable. In this way Vygotsky's explanation of play differs markedly from the instructional relationship he proposes in relation to the ZPD.

The notion of the ZPD as conceived within the relationship between instruction and development, invoking as it does the role of adult as tutor, has been applied widely to all learning situations, including play (see for example Wood and Attfield, 2005). Clearly there is much merit in considering the relationship between play and learning, and between teaching and play, in these terms. But perhaps we need also to consider ways that Vygotsky's theory of *play* (rather than *instruction* – our emphasis) can be accommodated within the contexts of schooling. How, for example, can we ensure that children have opportunities to develop their imaginative capacities – enacting their understanding of what it means to be a 'mother', for example – and to begin to separate action from meaning in their encounters with the props of play ('a stick becomes a horse'). Indeed it is this latter point that is most pertinent to role-play in school. We should perhaps ask how far we allow children the opportunity to create their own play contexts, to provide props which give scope for children to transform one object into another, and to play with peers.

Smilansky and sociodramatic play

Seminal in the field of role-play, or sociodramatic play as she terms it, is the work of Smilansky. Her research, discussed widely in the literature (see for example Kitson, 1997; Umek *et al.*, 1999; Wood and Attfield, 2005), demonstrates that sociodramatic play can enhance significantly the development of children's cognitive and social skills in educational settings. In adopting roles, children negotiate a consensus of meaning with their peers regarding the themes of their play and the concomitant nature of their roles. Smilansky identifies dramatic play as a distinct form of human play. Moreover, she makes an important distinction between *dramatic* play (an activity which involves make-believe and role-taking) and 'its more mature form' (1990: 3) *sociodramatic* play, which must also involve cooperation between at least two children.

Thus, Smilansky argued, in sociodramatic play children learn to take on another's perspective and to empathise with the feelings and experiences of others (Smilansky and Shefatya, 1990). The importance of Smilansky's research for educators can be summarised as follows. First, her work draws attention to the possibility that not all children may engage *naturally* in fantasy play and that social and cultural factors may be a significant determinant of the level and extent of such play. Second, although Smilansky located her work within a Piagetian developmental framework, she modified it in several important respects. She outlined four types of play behaviours, namely functional play, constructive play, dramatic play and games with rules. We give a brief description below of these play types in order to highlight the position of sociodramatic play in the overall scheme:

- Functional play involves repetition and imitation, and offers the child the opportunity for exploration of the environment.
- Constructive play appears in early childhood but may characterise play throughout childhood and even adulthood. It involves manipulation and exploration of the material world. It also involves the addition of a preconceived plan.
- Games with rules are divided into two distinct forms of games. First, there are table games such as dominoes, cards, etc. Second, there are physical games such as hide-and-seek and ball games. Both require children to accept the existence of rules and to modify their behaviours accordingly.
- Dramatic play is a distinct form of play with an important distinction between dramatic play (an activity which involves make-believe and role-taking) and its more mature form, sociodramatic play, which must also involve cooperation between at least two children.

(adapted from Smilansky and Shefatya, 1990: 2–3)

According to Smilansky, sociodramatic play incorporates the following features:

1   *Imitative role-play*: the child undertakes a make-believe role and expresses it in imitative action and or/verbalisation.
2   *Make-believe with regard to objects*: movements or verbal declarations and/or materials or toys are substituted for real objects.
3   *Make-believe with regard to actions and situations*: verbal descriptions are substituted for actions and situations.
4   *Persistence in the play episode*: the child continues within a role or the theme for at least ten minutes.
5   *Interaction*: there are at least two players interacting within the context of the play episode.
6   *Verbal communication*: there is some verbal interaction related to the play.

(Ibid: 24)

Smilansky offers a useful model for identifying this kind of play. Of particular interest to early childhood education in general and the project in particular is Smilansky's emphasis on the socially interactive and negotiated dimension of play. Indeed this is one of its principal strengths in children's learning and development. For children to 'experience human relationships actively by symbolic representation' is, within Smilansky's formulation, central to human play, and this view incorporates also the notion that adults can play a vital role in enhancing children's sociodramatic play and hence aid their cognitive development and academic achievement. It would seem, then, that cooperative role-play, the type of play most often seen in four- and five-year-olds, brings together both symbolic representation and social interaction in a potentially powerful context.

Transforming play? How school changes role-play

From a pedagogical perspective, cultural-ecological studies may offer a way of understanding children's role-play since they consider the play environment or context as significant in shaping children's experiences and perceptions. Play environments include the physical and social aspects of children's immediate settings, such as home, school, neighbourhood or playground. Cultural-ecological contexts, however, also include levels of influence beyond the settings children directly encounter. These broader influences include historical influences that affect the way in which, for example, play is perceived in a given period – its value and its place. They also include cultural and ideological beliefs that affect where play occurs and with whom, or the meaning that is attached to certain types of play within a cultural or sub-cultural group (Bloch and Pellegrini, 1989: 4). Ecological approaches, inspired in large part by the seminal conceptual and empirical work of Bronfenbrenner (1979), emphasise the study of behaviour in the natural context of everyday life and activity (Bloch and Pellegrini, 1989: 2) and, moreover, aim to highlight the powerful coercive forces of settings (or 'environmental press' as Garbarino (1989) describes it) on children and their teachers. Over time, individual behaviour tends to become congruent with the situational demands of the environment. Patterns of behaviour (such as free play) are reinforced or extinguished depending upon what the environment 'demands, punishes, or tolerates' (Garbarino, 1989: 20). The concept of 'environmental press' is an important one for the pedagogy of play in school. The physical characteristics and social patterns of the classroom interact and, as Garbarino notes, 'generate behaviour-modifying forces' (ibid.). The central point here is that the intrinsic characteristics of play are vulnerable to the contextual forces of social settings, such as the classroom, to teachers' pedagogical practice and children's responses to it.

Nancy King contends that 'Classroom play is never, simply, the free expression of children. It is always shaped in one direction or another by several classroom contexts' (1992: 47). Classroom contexts are themselves subdivided into physical, personal, social and curricular. *Physical context* includes the spatial and temporal dimensions, the organisation of the environment and the nature of resources. Under *personal context* King notes that children's individual characteristics, aptitudes, interests and skills will inevitably shape the nature of classroom events. Each child has a personal history, which they bring to their play, and which may shape their play choices. Ethnicity, gender and social circumstances will also influence children's play activity (see also Connolly 2006; Brooker, 2002; Steedman, 1987). By *social context*, King means 'the organisation of human relations, peer-group friendship network, the exercise of power and authority in the classroom' (1992: 47). The teacher and other adults in the classroom, their theories, values, attitudes and beliefs about play and learning may influence the way in which children play. Even when adults do not participate directly in play, they will influence it through the rules governing classroom action, their expectations, both implicit and explicit, and their language. *Curricular context* can determine the temporal and motivational nature of play. Issues such as how much time is available for play, its relation to more formal tasks and the extent to which play is valued in the classroom inevitably impact on children's perceptions of and responses to play activities. How much (or how little) structure is given to play activities, the level of involvement of the teacher and other adults and issues pertaining to access, frequency and choice have considerable bearing on how play develops in school.

Within historical contexts King refers to the role of tradition, theory, research findings, and changing attitudes to play throughout history, demonstrating that these interact to shape the ways in which we work in schools. She sketches out the historical contexts in which educators conduct their work, noting the way in which attitudes towards play have changed from one of 'rejection to idealisation and justification' (1992: 49). Dominant themes include play as the natural and innocent expression of the young, play as preparation for the demands of adulthood, and play as recreation. Play in school, King contends, may be an extension of such attitudes. Play is widely regarded as a natural activity of childhood, but equally play may be utilised in classrooms as a means by which to motivate children to participate in academic tasks (ibid.).

The final category in King's model of contexts influencing play in school – 'societal contexts' – deals with the impact of societal forces. She cites in particular play under extreme circumstances such as war and/or deprivation. There is evidence, she argues, to suggest that when they are placed in harsh and horrific conditions, children's play provides a counterbalance to the immediate social reality (1992: 51).

Role-play contexts in which children engage in imaginative and symbolic play provide important opportunities for children to exercise and develop their social competence. Thus how we provide for and support the development of symbolic and imaginative activity is of vital importance. Of particular interest in this project is the child's first year in school, essentially one of social orientation and adjustment. The reception class is the point at which children are 'received' into the structures of schooling and thus begin the process of becoming school pupils (Saunders, 1989; Willes, 1981). On starting school the child enters into a social and cultural world that may contrast sharply with the world of home and pre-school settings (Corsaro, 1997; Brooker, 2002). Even when policies are developed to support children in the process of transition from one setting to another, they are inevitably exposed to a welter of cultural information that may be overwhelming and difficult to process (Corsaro, 1997) and that runs counter to their experiences at home. Brooker (2006) notes the ways in which early childhood practices contribute to children's developing identities around gender and ethnicity. Moreover, children's perceptions of the social conventions associated with ownership, possession and sharing, derived from their early experiences, may not be compatible with the interactive demands of the early childhood setting. Clearly the ways in which play is organised and presented to children need also to acknowledge such differences in perception on the part of the children. With this in mind, approaches to role-play that merely reproduce dominant adult perceptions of the 'real world' are unlikely to allow for children to find and express their own meaning in their play. The transformative rather than purely reproductive quality of role-play can allow children to find their own and collective meaning. In this way, role-play that is open-ended and flexible 'may allow cultural hegemony to be turned on its head' (Guss, 2004).

Questions have been raised about the value of structuring the role-play environment according to adult-selected themes and resources, and the increased promotion of adult intervention specifically to guide curriculum learning through play. The main criticisms appear to be centred on the over-use of realistic props which, particularly for children aged from three to five, do not require the same level of agreement among players that is demanded by more open-ended materials (Trawick-Smith, 1998). Skills such as negotiation, for example, are less likely to be required when real-life props are provided than when children transform objects, from say 'a stick to a horse' (Vygotsky, 1978). Other studies that have considered specifically the impact of classroom practices on children's social development (Corsaro, 1985, 1997; Avgitidou, 1997; McLean, 1991; Trawick-Smith, 1998) suggest that over-prescriptive and highly structured play environments militate against the kind of peer culture and activity that would lead to the development of social skills in the context of children's friendships. For young children in particular, peer group play may serve an important function in helping children to make sense of such information and to become socialised into the structures of schooling. However, school is also the place 'where the young child's largely self-directed exploration of things, people and situations is displaced by a more systematic induction into social patterns of meaning' (Parker-Rees, 1999: 61), so we are left to consider the tension between the child's natural and powerful propensity to play in ways that transform and find new meanings, often in familiar objects, situations and relationships, and the pedagogical imperative to reproduce real life – the café, the shop, the doctor's surgery – so that requirements in literacy and numeracy can be met. The use of highly structured role-play environments raises some important questions about the extent to which children in early childhood settings have the opportunity to exercise choice and to make decisions about the nature and direction of their play (Rogers, 2000). Role-play may be structured temporally, thematically and materially and the practice of linking role-play explicitly to school-based learning, in particular to literacy, may be related more to the need to justify its presence in school than to any specific pedagogical rationale (Trawick-Smith, 1998; Bergen, 2002). We do need to consider carefully the motivations underpinning the organisation of the play environment.

To what extent are children exercising their intellectual, social and imaginative capacities in their play? If, as these studies suggest, an over-emphasis on adult-devised themes may in fact dissuade children from pursuing their own play needs, and, moreover, an over-use of realistic props and materials may also limit children's social interactions and imaginative activity, we should perhaps reconsider the balance between the product-orientated demands of school-based learning and the process-orientated potential of play. Against this background, it would be all too easy to down-play the physical, social and affective qualities of play or recreation, and to neglect the imaginative, playful and creative dispositions inherent in play, in order to substitute in its place a highly prescribed, externally evaluated, purposeful play regime.

Conclusion

The capacity to engage in shared pretence, to enact the part of something or someone else, is a profound and uniquely human activity. The ability to engage in this type of play develops rapidly from birth, emerging most fully in children aged from three to five. Role-play appears to support a wide range of important skills and abilities that contribute to later learning. From a pedagogical standpoint, research suggests that for children in early childhood settings, including reception classes, it is vitally important to provide ample opportunities for this kind of play. We can summarise the main points of this chapter as follows:

- Role-play encourages representational thinking.
- Role-play helps children to develop perspective-taking skills (seeing another person's point of view).
- Role-play displays children's language competence.
- Role-play involves problem-solving.
- Role-play encourages turn-taking and negotiation.

- For role-play to develop, children need to communicate the play themes to one another, moving frequently between reality and fantasy/pretence.
- Children therefore need to be able to hold notions of reality *and* fantasy at the same time.
- In role-play, children need at any one time to engage a complex number of aspects including play mates, toys and props, time and space.
- In role-play, children have a strong desire to affiliate with one another and to maintain peer interactions (Corsaro, 1985).
- In role-play, children have a strong desire to self-generate themes.
- Children need to interpret and use complex cues from the play environment and from the players (gestures, facial expressions).
- Children experience close proximity to others and develop early friendships through role-play (Dunn, 2004).
- Role-play helps to establish and sustain children's peer culture, which begins to take on great significance in children aged from three to five.
- Role-play offers children social allegiance in the context of living in the powerful world of adult authority (Corsaro, 1997; Guss, 2005).

This chapter has outlined the ways in which children from birth develop the capacity to engage in the uniquely human activity that is role-play. It has highlighted key aspects of role-play that we might observe in children's activity in the classroom. What follows now in Chapter 3 is an account of the research process, design and methodology which will set into context the discussion of the data.

Researching young children's perspectives

A multi-method approach

Background to the project

The overall aim of the project was to undertake a sustained and detailed study of children's role-play activity in order to understand more fully the relationship between teachers' provision (the *offered* curriculum) on the one hand, and children's responses to that provision (the *received* curriculum) on the other. How, for example, do teachers organise this type of play in terms of thematic and material structures, grouping practices, modes of access, and adult intervention? In what ways does such provision impact on the nature of children's role-play activity in terms of its generic characteristics such as make-believe, social interaction between peers, communication and transformation of meaning?

With this in mind the project set out to:

1   examine the ways in which teachers plan for and organise role-play in reception classes;
2   examine the ways in which children respond to different types of role-play provision in reception classes.
3   understand children's perspectives on their experiences of role-play in school;
4   develop methodologies for studying children's role-play in early child-hood settings.

Two key principles underpinned the project. First, a collaborative relationship with the participating teachers and children was central, so that we could build a relationship of trust and mutual sharing of ideas. Second, the sociocultural concept that children are active agents, who may be restricted or encapsulated by social structures (Prout and James, 1997) guided our research ethos and approach. Thus we were wholly committed to the involvement of the children in sharing their perspectives on role-play. Indeed it is this latter aspect that is methodologically innovatory in the field. It is well documented that, traditionally, young children have been cast in the role of subjects of research rather than active participants (Clark and Moss, 2001), and while the number of published studies of young children's perspectives of early childhood services has increased both in the UK and elsewhere, there are still relatively few studies of young children's reflections on their experiences of playing and learning in the school context: a situation we wanted to rectify. Whilst undertaking research with young children may be methodologically challenging, we were of the opinion that 'children from a surprisingly early age can understand the basic elements of the research process and their role within it if this information is presented in an age appropriate manner' (Thompson, 1992: 60).

Sample

The focus is on provision for children in the final year of the Foundation Stage: in other words aged four to five in each setting. There were two main reasons for selecting this age group. First, research indicates that children are particularly receptive to imaginative and symbolic activity at this age (Piaget, 1962; Van Oers, 1994), and second, the provision of high-quality play-based activity has been shown repeatedly to be particularly problematic in reception classes (Bennett and Kell, 1989; Bennett *et al.*, 1997; Rogers, 2000). Collaboration with a group of interested teachers was established through a questionnaire study of teachers' perceptions of role-play. The final sample consisted of three reception classes of primary schools in the south-west of England:

- a reception and Year 1 mixed class in a rural primary school;
- a reception class in a primary school in a small town;
- an early years unit in a large, urban first school.

Participant teachers were selected for their interest in improving the quality of role-play in their classrooms. Whilst many of their approaches around aspects of their pedagogical practices do not necessarily reflect a 'top-down' teacher approach to decision-making processes (Christensen and James, 2002; Mayall, 1994 in Powell *et al.*, 2006), what these teachers offered was some insight into how things could be if children were co-creators of their learning environment.

Ethical considerations

Strict ethical procedures endorsed by the University of Plymouth and the British Educational Research Association were adhered to throughout. When undertaking research with children within any institutional or formalised set-ting, ethics must always lie at the centre of the research agenda. The perceived vulnerability of children which encompasses their need for protection, coupled with the issue of informed consent, means that the researcher needs to be clear that the child can understand what they are consenting to and are able to understand what may be expected of them. Arguably, the younger the child, the more problematic this becomes, particularly where the research is carried out within an institutional setting where children's power to say 'no' without sanction is limited.

Sieber (1993) suggests that ethics in research relate to 'the application of a system of moral principles to prevent harming or wronging others, to promote the good, to be respectful, and to be fair' (see Morrow and Richards, 1996). The absolute baseline according to Davis (1998) must be that children are able to understand that they have the power to withdraw from the research at any time. When undertaking research with children researchers already find themselves entering an ethical minefield. For example, do children fully understand what is being asked of them? In this research we were in project schools for the period of a school year, so we were able to build relationships with the children and we were open and frank with them about our role. As can be seen later in this chapter, we were challenged regularly by the children about our role and about what we were doing in their classroom, ensuring that we maintained an open and honest relationship with them.

The children were selected in negotiation with the teachers, and the children who participated in group activities with us chose play project names (pseudonyms) to which we refer throughout the book. Thus all real names of the children and the teachers have been substituted with alternatives. Across the three schools, eighty children participated in the study in the first term, rising to 144 in the second term. The number of adults who participated consisted of six teachers (all female) and six teaching assistants (five female, one male). Seventy-one visits were made over the school year, each lasting half a school day. The ethnic profile of two of the three areas was 98.3 per cent white, while that of the third area, in a more urban location, was 96.1 per cent white (2001 Census).

Methodology

The research is qualitative, drawing upon the principles of ethnography. Ethnography is 'a distinct type of research where the knowledge that is produced depends on the researcher taking part in close social interaction with informants over extensive periods of time' (Christensen, 2004: 166). Thus in its principal form it involves overt and sometimes covert participation in people's daily lives, watching, listening and asking questions, collecting available data to illuminate the detail which surrounds the focus of the research (Hammersley and Atkinson, 2006). The equivalent of ten days was spent in each of the three classrooms during each school term (one day or two half days per week) over a period of a school year, with the aim of identifying features of good practice as well as areas for development.

A qualitative approach also provides a useful means of addressing personal meaning. Such an approach is also appropriate if the researcher needs to target the data to the interviewees' particular interests, for example if the need arose to explore a specific rather than a general point. Whilst this may also be seen to be a weakness in terms of accuracy and validity, it is recognised that all methods of research are open to interviewer bias (Morgan, 1997). In the context of this research we took an interpretivist approach: the initial aim being to employ the Weberian concept of *verstehen*, i.e. to understand the social world from the perspective of the children, living, negotiating and understanding the structures in which they operate.

Methods

In order to elicit the children's perspectives we developed a range of child-focused methods (see for example Clark and Moss, 2001), taking into account their age and ability to communicate. This meant that we did not necessarily rely on methods that required children to write or speak. In practical terms when working with younger children a range of creative methods are often required to sustain interest and to appeal to the methods of communication that many children are familiar with and enjoy using (James *et al.*, 1998; Morrow and Richards, 1996; Hill *et al.*, 1996). Using a creative and intra-method approach also offered children the freedom to explore and express their own ideas on a topic whilst having the reassurance of their peers within the group who were working with them at the same time. Additionally we wanted to minimise the risk of bias likely from an over-reliance on one type of data collection (Morrow and Richards, 1996). Therefore, using multiple methods enabled us to access data from a range of different perspectives. Data were collected in the following ways:

- In-depth, semi-structured interviews were conducted with each teacher at the start of the project. The interviews explored how teachers currently provided for role-play, how they believed role-play contributes to children's learning in the Foundation Stage, the nature of their function, and any problems they may have encountered in providing for role-play.
- Participant and non-participant observations were conducted of significant features of classroom context. In particular, these included details of class routine, grouping practices, modes of access to play, and thematic content.
- Videotaped episodes of role-play were recorded for more detailed consideration.
- Participant observation of small group work was carried out.

- Participant and non-participant observation of role-play was undertaken.
- Photographs were taken by both the children and the researchers.
- Conversations with children were engaged in.
- Children were asked to draw their favourite role-play themes; role-play scenarios and stories were noted.

Transcripts and field notes were read and re-read by the research team and key themes were identified. Drawings and photographs were shared with the children, engendering detailed discussions with the researchers about how they were interpreting aspects of their role-play provision. Using photographs also enabled the researchers to comprehend the children's understandings of their play themes on different levels; for example, 'listening as a way of relating; [as a] space for critique [and] as a means of inclusion and participation' (Clarke et al., 2005). We also found that children enjoyed using the cameras, and it thus proved to be a method that was not only inclusive but also highly valued both collectively as an artefact of the project and as an individual contribution. For example, the following extract is taken from our field notes after one of the children had been given her photographs (we agreed that the children could choose two photographs to keep from those they had taken):

> Today I took in some photographs that Annie had taken. I gave them to her and she immediately took them off to the student teacher and said 'I took these, she gave me these' [pointing to me]. The teacher did not really understand the context of what Annie was saying. Annie went off to put her photographs in her book bag, showing other children along the way and explaining them as she went, 'This is me and 'punzel, this is her crown'. Dan then came over to me and said, 'Can I have mine?' It seems that the children really do value having something given to them that they have been involved with and something they had a free choice in deciding what their photographic subject matter would be.
>
> (Field notes)

We would, therefore, concur with Clark and Moss that 'cameras offer young children the opportunity to produce a finished product in which they can take pride ... photographs can offer a powerful new language for young children' (2001: 24). Our methods were designed to allow children to think and talk about role-play and were varied enough to allow as many children as possible to participate, irrespective of their ability to articulate their thoughts verbally or in writing. We also compiled detailed field notes from sustained observation of children engaged in role-play. All themes, both major and minor, were checked against the data. Data findings were shared and discussed with project teachers informally in the course of the research, and in project meetings.

In short, we felt that ethnographic methods were a particularly useful medium for engaging with children and, albeit temporarily, provided the opportunity to engage with the ways in which children construct, discuss and make sense of differing aspects of their everyday lives. For us, we saw ethnography as a useful way of understanding 'how people make sense of the world in their everyday life' (Hammersley and Atkinson, 2006: 2), or in this research, how children are making sense of their everyday world(s) through their role-play. Using focus groups and other visual task-based methods that are seen as a positive way of engaging effectively with children (Prosser, 1998) also enabled the data to be located within a wider sociological framework but without losing their child-centric view.

A note about research ethos

Traditionally, doing research with children has been seen, in some senses, as a risky enterprise (Hood *et al.*, 1996), but to be able to give children the chance to have a voice and express their thoughts and feelings on their lives can be empowering both for the children and researchers alike. As Prout concludes, 'only through different participative mechanisms at all levels of society can different children's interests and experiences have a chance of being heard' (2000: 10), and this was the premise on which we based the project. Thus from its inception the project was a collaborative endeavour between the children, the research team and the schools. Further, we regarded the children as experts and agents in their own lives, and aspired to embed the research in current and future practice (Clark and Moss, 2001). We were also mindful that how we view children's position in the wider social world is clearly going to affect the methods that are adopted and the interpretation of the data that are collected. As Morrow and Richards suggest, 'in terms of methodology, researchers need to think carefully about the standpoint from which they are studying children, and the ethical implications of that standpoint' (1996: 100). Our standpoint was thus to place the children at the centre of the research and not get too caught up with the concerns and pressures of the prevailing adult agendas. In short, we wanted to listen to children on 'many levels' (Clarke and Moss, 2001). Quite how we can convey this in print remains a considerable challenge for us, but in keeping with our approach to the research itself, we will endeavour to keep the children's voices at the centre of this book.

Reflexivity

Consideration of both the research topic and the ontological positioning of the researcher is a key part of ethnography, ensuring that the researcher reflexively monitors her own position as the researcher as well as the research process itself. Arguably it is better to acknowledge bias rather than to hide behind a mask of objectivity (Cooper and Stevenson, 1997). In social research, how can we have lived and continue to live and engage in a similar world to those that we research, and not adhere to certain values or hold beliefs about why things may be as they are? As Hammersley and Atkinson point out, 'social researchers are part of the social world they study' (1995: 16). Trying to isolate data that are uncontaminated by the researcher is, according to Hammersley and Atkinson, a futile exercise in as far as all data involve theoretical pre-suppositions.

The whole concept of aspiring to or achieving value-free research has caused considerable debate since the advent of the social sciences. Arguably we all have a linguistic currency of values and these are certainly difficult to define universally. Some values may be moral and open to subjectivity but even a value that can be measured in monetary terms may still be interpreted in different ways. Weber (1949) argued that social science should and could be value-free; the key for Weber was in *verstehen* sociology where we can understand values without making value judgements. Weber believed that it was possible to acknowledge the value system at the heart of the research but still have the ability to put personal values on the subject to one side.

The real issue as to what role 'values' may or may not play in any research project, we would suggest, is that researchers should be clear about their own value bases compared with those of the people they may be researching, where thir own boundaries lie and where the participants' boundaries may be at any given point in the research relationship. This can be achieved by being open and reflexive about the methods used and the intent of the research agenda. The concept of reflexivity is a critical part of the qualitative research process and many researchers (particularly within feminist methodologies) acknowledge that our subjectivity is part of our biography, which we cannot externalise or escape from (nor should we want to). The important issue is to be aware of it and to reflect on our own practice (Stanley, 1990). Arguing persuasively, Lather (1995) suggests that reflexivity and critique are the two essential skills that need to be developed on the journey towards cultural demystification: 'Research which encourages self and social understanding ... requires research designs that allow us as researchers to reflect on how our value commitments insert themselves into our empirical work' (1995: 301). In the role of researcher we never enter the research from an uncontaminated perspective: our experiences, our gender, our social class position and our ethnic origins will have all been constructed within the social and cultural discourses available to us in the society in which we live. Our role(s) and identities as adults have been created through a particular experience of childhood, all of which shape our understanding of others. In the project, we were open, honest and transparent with all those participating in the research, and as researchers we regularly reflected upon what we brought to the research setting and the ways in which we approached the research. We had different experiences and perspectives (an educationalist and a sociologist) and needed to be continually reflexive in terms of what we were seeing and hearing and what that might say about the data that were being generated.

Validity and reliability

Adopting qualitative methods as a means of enquiry into the social worlds of others has traditionally left the researcher open to issues of bias and the problem of subjectivity and interpretation. We recognised the need to address these concerns in the early stages of the project. There are also issues about what data are included and, it follows, excluded. The project generated large amounts of data and it is not possible to include them all. Implicit in these criticisms is that data yielded from qualitative methods are not scientific or valid. Validity and reliability are key elements in the research process as qualitative methodology relies heavily on interpretation. De Vaus (1996) suggests that interpretation is another problem associated with developing valid indicators of the meaning of people's responses. In addition, when working with children we believed that valid accounts of children's attitudes and experiences can only really be obtained by talking directly with the children, as Mahon *et al.* (1996) suggest that adults such as parents and teachers cannot give valid accounts of children's social worlds. Moreover, as we identified earlier, the younger a child is, the less likely it is that they will be engaged in participatory research (Clark *et al.*, 2005), a situation we wanted to remedy not least because we wanted to understand role-play from a four-year-old's perspective.

Approaching research with young children

Entering in to the research we were mindful that throughout modernity children in Western culture have, until perhaps recently, been seen but not heard. Adults such as parents and teachers, whilst often doing what they do for the very best of reasons, are arguably caught within the discourses of wider social, political and educational viewpoints as well as their own experiential views on child-rearing practices. As adults we may lose sight of the fact that children's experiences of the world are not what adults think they are. Eliciting details of those experiences is a major research task in itself. Although there have been shifts at an academic and a political level, there are still areas at policy, social and pedagogical levels where children are not afforded the freedom and autonomy to be heard (Hill *et al.*, 2004; Prout, 2001). As Lansdown suggests, 'we simply do not have a culture of listening to children' (1994: 38). The problem is compounded further by the fact that when undertaking research with children there is a double-bind in terms of the power imbalance: first between the researcher and interviewee, and second between the adult and the child. Whilst the ideal would be to neutralise all power imbalances, Alderson (1995) suggests that the research either reinforces the imbalance or questions it. Other approaches indicate that it is inescapable that children will not be affected by the inequalities between them and the researcher (Mayall, 1996); further, Hood *et al.* (1996) suggest that the social mismatch between the adult interviewer and the child subject may be lessened when children participate as part of a group with their peers. Jenks (2000: 70) takes a much more definitive stance when he concludes that researchers are always adults and they are always different from children because they are socially clustered in generational forms. Alternatively, others suggest a shift from seeing power as residing in people and social positions towards viewing power as embedded in the process of 'doing' the research (Christensen, 2004: 167).

All social researchers have to grapple with the thorny issue of the power dynamics inherent in the research process. Working with children, however, blurs the issue even further as all researchers have been children and live within an experiential framework constructed through notions of childhood. Therefore we arrived as adult researchers with our biographies that had built upon our experiences and had been filtered through the lens of our under-standing of childhood (Mayall, 1994; Thorne, 1993). Whatever methodological standpoint you adopt within the research process, at some point 'children have to leave their interpretation of their own [thoughts] to another age group whose interests are potentially at odds with those of them-selves. This is a sociology of knowledge problem, which so far is almost unexplored' (Qvortrup, 1994: 6). However, we believe that children can help with the social presentation of other children by offering a 'collective' account of how they view their lives (Mayall, 2000). Small groups also help to neu-tralise the power imbalance that there may be in a one-to-one interview between an adult researcher and a child (Mahon *et al.*, 1996; James, 1999).

The role of the researcher

One solution that is offered to the epistemological positioning of children is to take the 'least adult role' (Mandell, 1991), which suggests that researchers distance themselves from the position as adult in all aspects of their role other than their physical size. Mandell's position has been questioned and critiqued (see James *et al.*, 1998; Harden *et al.*, 2000); however, from our perspective we tried to adopt Mandell's 'least adult' role in terms of not wanting to assume an authority role, or to be construed as being 'teachers'. Hence we asked the children to refer to us by our first names and purposely avoided responding to children's requests to mediate conflict, as we were repeatedly asked to do; for example, 'Julie, tell him that he's not allowed to do that ...' (Kitty, aged four). In short, we did not want to take on the 'teacher' or 'teaching assistant' role in which intervention was often about mediation, interference and disruption, which in many cases dissipated the play (see also Christensen, 2004: 169).

Given that the children were all having their first 'formal' experience of school life combined with the routines and procedures of the classroom environment, maintaining a 'least adult' role was both challenging for and challenged by the children on a regular basis. Children often queried what the researcher was doing, where she lived, what she 'did' (where she worked) and what she was writing in her notebook. Some children asked the researcher to read to them what had been written down, and on some occasions she was told by the children to write down particular things in her notebook. Reflecting on this we believe this was just a means by which the children could gain some control over the process and 'test' whether the researchers really were listening and engaged with what they were saying.

There were also times when the children 'used' the researcher as an 'adult authority' figure even when she was not in that role. In the following example Christopher wants to take the lid off a tray but Wayne does not want him to do that. Unable to persuade him to stop, Wayne tries to use adult leverage to steer the outcome and says: 'Julie's watching you'. It was at times like these that any available adult would be called upon by children to affect the outcome of a particular course of action.

When we started the research we had the best of intentions based on our own research experiences, other researchers' experiences, and the school environment where the research was taking place, to adopt a 'least adult' approach. With hindsight we now realise that to eradicate generational differences between adults and children is not possible within the research setting (Mayall, 2000), certainly not in an educational setting where adult authority is so acute. As can be seen from the description below, one of the researchers had a very powerful example of how children are drawing on the discourses in which they operate to make sense of adults' roles in the world or in this case in their school setting. It also offered a lucid example of how research participants can reflect the way in which they are 'constructing' the researcher.

About six months into the project, one school was involved in a sponsored walk. About half the reception-class children were involved in this out-of-school activity. The remaining children were left to undertake various classroom activities. During one particular activity – observational drawing – the researcher was sitting with a group of girls whilst they drew a piece of fruit. The teacher had popped out of the classroom. Alice had finished her drawing and said to the researcher, 'Can I draw another one?' Staying in 'least adult' role the researcher replied, 'I'm not sure, Alice, perhaps you could ask Ms Fields when she comes back'. Anna replied, 'You can tell me, you're a teacher'. Startled at her response (having done so much to take the 'least adult' role) the researcher replied, 'Alice, I'm not a teacher'. Millie, sitting opposite, continued with her drawing and without looking up said, 'No she's not a teacher, she's a mummy'. The researcher was taken aback by both responses, having worked with the children for many months and firmly believed she was in a 'least adult' role. One of that researcher's field notes also illustrates the difficulties of how you are constructed by others irrespective of how you might be constructing yourself:

> Clearly, from a methodological standpoint children are offering feedback that they do not see me as 'least adult'. I might see myself as that but they are still looking to me to make 'adult' decisions and as having the power to resolve their conflicts. So 'least adult' arguably is not tenable in a school environment where adult authority is so acute?
>
> (Field notes)

On reflection and after subsequent discussions with colleagues, however, we could see that for four-year-old children, many adult women of the researcher's age that they encounter are either a teacher or a mummy; that is their experience of the world. As researchers, this was a salutary lesson in that no matter how much you try to position yourself or adopt a particular methodological standpoint, research participants, whether they are children or adults, are 'positioning' you according to the discourses within which they are operating.

As Alice's and Millie's comments so clearly demonstrate, the 'best' we can attain is, as Mayall suggests, to work with generational issues rather than just to down-play them. What Mayall asks for as a researcher is for children 'through their own unique knowledge ... to help [her] as an adult to understand childhood' (2000: 122). On this basis, the children helped us as adults to understand more fully their experiences of role-play within their classroom settings.

Children's responses to the research process

Both directly and indirectly over the school year, we gained feedback from the children about how they were relating to us, the researchers, and the research process. In the early stages of the research, as the children were getting to know us and we were getting to know them, we were very careful to ask for access to observe their play. On several occasions children said 'no'. As researchers we felt this demonstrated that at that stage we were clearly 'outsiders' as children would not say 'no' to teachers in the same way. In fact we observed situations where children did say no to teachers and got a punitive response. For some children (at such a young age) being able to say 'no' to an adult when they were learning how to interact with adults in the classroom environment was probably confusing. Children did not always refuse verbally, but it was quite clear when we were not welcome. In one particular setting at a very early stage of the study (the second week) before the children were fully familiar with the researchers, one of the researchers was observing Eve's and Liam's 'Small Island' play from a distance. Eve was narrating a story about the dinosaurs on the island but due to the noise levels in the classroom it was becoming increasingly difficult to hear what she was saying. The researcher moved closer to the island to try to pick up on the story but both Liam and Eve moved away to another activity. Liam's and Eve's withdrawal from the play was as a direct result of the researcher moving closer and the children had made it very clear that at this stage they were not prepared to have an 'outsider' infiltrating their play space, a good example of children making their own decisions about participation (or not) in research (Davis, 1998). Although not articulated, this was a clear sign of resistance through withdrawal by these children.

Concluding comments

Working with the children in the ways outlined above was methodologically challenging and highly instructive. Participating in the children's activities over a full school year gave us invaluable insights into their experiences of role-play and of school. A myriad questions have been raised as a result of adopting this approach, which would benefit from further study. Understanding the children as individual personalities, watching them develop their friendship groups, embedding themselves into school life with all the routines and rules that entails, and their interaction with the adults around them could probably only have been achieved by adopting this method.

Undertaking observations was a very successful method and whilst there are limitations with any method, watching children negotiate, interact and play produced hard evidence of the complexities of trying to understand young children's behaviour in relation to the wider social structures in which they operate, e.g. school, peer groups and with adults. Observation for short periods of time offers adults (as the outsiders) a snapshot of young children's school lives, and the building of a relationship with the children over time produced data that we probably could not have obtained through more talk-based methods. Young children do not yet have all the tools and the language to express themselves as clearly as researchers might wish. Whilst it would be foolish to think that one's presence as an outsider is forgotten, the children did in the context of this research enter their own worlds of discussion, negotiations, thoughts and feelings for extended periods. Whilst children are discussing ideas with each other it could be argued that this allows the researcher a glimpse into their lives and their worlds as they live and negotiate their individual pathways through it. As Mayall asserts, children can help 'adults tap into one of the means whereby, through talking with each other, children firm up knowledge and learn more about aspects of their social worlds' (2000: 133).

We started from the premise that children have much to tell us as adults if only we would take the time to listen. As subsequent chapters will demonstrate, with careful listening (on many levels), the children in this study clearly articulated verbally and sometimes via other means their understanding and experiences of teachers' role-play provision in their early years environment. These four-year-olds' perspectives offered powerful insights into an area of children's experience. This also enabled the teachers to reflect on practice and consider future provision of role-play in their classroom.

Chapter 4

Teachers' perspectives on role-play

In Chapter 2, we concluded that young children demonstrate an inherent capacity to engage in role-play and that it is a central feature of their early development. Few would dispute this. Yet how such insights are to be translated into pedagogical practice has presented the field with some of its most enduring challenges. We established at the outset that the overarching aim of the project was to explore the relationship between role-play and pedagogy, between teachers' provision and children's responses to that provision and that the children's perspectives on these matters are at the heart of our concerns. But our discussion would not be complete without some consideration of what their teachers thought about role-play and how they organised their classrooms accordingly. The introduction of the Foundation Stage in 2000, and with it greater official recognition of how play contributes to young children's education, was already well established by the time we began working with our teachers in 2003. According to the documentation, all early childhood settings are required to offer children appropriate educational experiences within the remit of the *Curriculum Guidance for the Foundation Stage* (CFGS) (QCA 2000), which endorses a play-based, informal curriculum that is responsive to the developmental, social and physical needs of children in this age group. In spite of these significant changes to policy regarding the educational experiences of children below statutory school age, an extensive piece of research conducted by Adams *et al.* (2004) noted a range of continuing problems for teachers and children in reception classes, particularly in relation to fulfilling the requirements of the CGFS to provide a play-based active learning environment. Top-down pressure from the SATs (Standard Assessment Tasks), a target-driven culture in primary schools, leagues tables and concomitant expectations from colleagues and parents placed many reception-class teachers under continued pressure to prepare children for formal learning. In a similar vein to the study by Adams *et al.* (2004), Fisher notes the pressure exerted on reception-class teachers from the National Literacy Strategy (NLS), where the emphasis is on the so-called 'literacy hour' rather than developmentally appropriate practice (2000: 134).

Against this background, we describe teachers' perspectives on the place of role-play in early learning. We offer two distinct forms of data: first, data generated from a questionnaire, based upon Smilansky's survey of teachers' attitudes to sociodramatic play (Smilansky and Shefatya, 1990), the purpose being to identify key areas for investigation and provide a wider context for the classroom-based project. The second set of data is from interviews conducted with teachers in the three project schools. These case studies were selected from a larger sample of teachers who completed the questionnaire and whose settings represented the range of reception classes in the area in terms of size, location and class composition.

Summary of findings of the questionnaire survey

Two geographical locations were chosen to conduct the survey in: one in the south-east of England and the other in the south-west of England. In total 178 questionnaires were returned, representing a response rate of 55 per cent. The sample can be broken down as shown in Table 4.1.

The value of role-play

In the questionnaire, role-play was regarded as an important aspect of early years provision for children. Some teachers stated that role-play was vital and central to children's school experience because it helped them to develop social skills, to cooperate with their peers, to interact with others and generally to improve their language development. Role-play was also seen as an ideal medium through which children could express their creativity and develop their imaginations. The 'added value' of role-play was that it could be used to reinforce learning and was also a popular activity for the children and one in which they could explore and express other aspects of their personalities. For example:

> Quiet children, shy with adults can be surprisingly forward with their peers.

> Relationships often flourish during role-play situations; children with integration problems can sometimes find their 'niche' here.

Table 4.1 Type of educational provision in the two areas studied

	Primary	Nursery	First[a]	Primary/nursery	Total[b]
South-west England	63	6	3	0	72
South-east England	53	37	7	7	104

Notes:
a First school – children aged 5–8 years
b Two of the 178 submitted questionnaires did not specify geographical location

Opportunities for role-play

Across all schools that responded, it was evident that the stage of education children were at was the main factor in the number of opportunities they were given to engage in role-play. The majority of teachers stated that younger children have the opportunity to engage in role-play more than older children do. For example, the opportunities declined in reception compared with nursery, followed by a significant decrease in Year 1 compared with reception, (although this cannot be accurately quantified, as a specific question was not asked about changes in role-play opportunities). Role-play had disappeared altogether by the time children had entered Year 2. The difference between the opportunities available for role-play between reception and Year 1 children was significant: teachers were aware that in Year 1, pressure from the National Curriculum greatly reduced children's opportunity to engage in role-play.

> Year 1s, no. National Curriculum does not seem to allow unless topic time can be built into the curriculum.

> ...constraints of the NC in mixed age class make this less easy.

As well as the impact of curriculum, role-play opportunities were also restricted by the number of children who were allowed to go into the role-play area at any one time; ensuring that all children had access to the area further impacted on the actual number of opportunities for role-play. In this study just over half of the respondents (51 per cent) said that they expected children to be in the role-play area at some time during the week. In theory, role-play is available to all children on a regular basis; however, the constraints that operate within the classroom mean that in practice children's opportunities to role-play are greatly reduced and this is a source of frustration to adults and children alike. Some respondents stated that role-play was a 'free' choice but many responses indicated that adults sanctioned the choice; therefore it could be argued that it was not a free choice but a restricted choice:

> Free choice but adults ensure rotation.

> The children choose for themselves, though I make sure that all children have a turn so I limit the numbers in the area to ensure that the play is constructive and not too noisy.

> Free choice unless necessary to ensure some children do not dominate the area, we would then choose those playing there.

Several respondents made the point that some children either don't like or are reluctant to role-play and should not be forced in to it. This last point was a strong theme that several teachers commented on. They clearly felt that children should be *encouraged* rather than *coerced* or forced into activities they felt uncomfortable with. A selection of responses to the question 'do you expect children in your class to play in the role-play area at some time during the week?' follows:

> No – some may not enjoy the experience but like watching, curiosity eventually overcomes them.

> No – it's not appropriate for everyone.

> No, some children do not enjoy this type of play.

> No. Some children are not happy with something different – particularly children who have not been to playgroup or nursery.

> No it's their choice most do play in either home corner, RP area because I would not want to force this type of activity on to them as they may feel it is something they don't need, don't enjoy or are not interested in.

The theme of the role-play area was important in stimulating and maintaining children's engagement with role-play. As children's interests wane, ideas often become stale and result in fewer children choosing role-play. Teachers changed the role-play themes regularly, in accordance with their curriculum plans. The range of themes on offer to children included some that required children to engage in more unusual fantasy worlds; for example, underwater cave or tropical rainforest. However, the most frequent themes reported were real world themes:

- shop
- hospital
- post office
- café
- veterinary surgery
- travel agency
- doctor's surgery
- Chinese restaurant.

Teachers' comments on the purposes underlying their provision of role-play varied, including viewing it as a medium through which children could start to make sense of the adult world around them, and as an opportunity for children to work through anxieties and problems that they may be experiencing at home or in school. As Cohen (1993) notes, a main psychological benefit of play can be in emotional expression and healing. Erikson (1963) also argues that early play rehearses difficult situations that children may well have to face in practical and emotional domains (sorrow, anger, blame, etc.) and further suggests that the dramatisation that takes place in play can also be a crucial dynamic in the maturational process, and that children can, through play, learn to express and manage their emotions. Many respondents appeared to support this view, citing the principal value of role-play as a vehicle through which children could express aspects of their personalities beyond what they knew or had learned, assume another role, or explore other roles in the 'safety' of a role-play setting:

> To develop an awareness of oneself in relation to others – to foster cooperation. To enable troubled children to act out their anxieties.

> Role-play enables children to enrich their experiences; to be 'someone else'; to pretend (maybe that they are still a baby, especially if there is a new baby at home); to act out, albeit unknowingly, emotional problems and difficulties.

> Seeing the world from the point of view of others. Acting out situations which [children] may find difficult in real life.

> ... acting out various real life situations and can be therapeutic for children with problems.

The questionnaire data highlighted that the majority of teachers who responded had not received any training in how to develop a child's ability to engage in role-play, and nor had they received training in assessing or evaluating children's play ability. Conversely, nursery staff (non-teaching) had received formal training in these elements of children's development. Teachers' lack of training may lead to a view of play that is derived from curriculum perspectives rather than reflecting children's understanding, thoughts and feelings about their experiences. Some teachers requested further training in setting up role-play areas and understanding how it contributes to children's learning and development:

> More help to set up different play situations as most of the children entering this school cannot play properly.

> To intervene and lead the children's play on, if they are not playing appropriately.

If we accept the proposal in Chapter 2, that children aged three to five engage in more pretend play than any other kind of play (Corsaro, 1997) and that shared pretence is an inherently 'human' achievement, it may be worthwhile to ponder what is meant by 'unable to play properly' or 'appropriately'. Other teachers identified a number of key issues for future development, including space, resources and training:

> More space, more equipment, more ideas for role-play which can be done without teacher intervention.

> Literature on role-play would be helpful particularly when trying to find unusual ways of reinforcing role-play area.

Constraints on role-play

From the survey data it was possible to ascertain key constraints on classroom practice. These were in evidence in school rather than in nursery settings and particularly in mixed age group classes. Most notable in the data was the need to *contain* role-play in view of the noise levels it generated, lack of classroom space (71 per cent) and the boisterous nature of role-play. These factors were highlighted as particularly disruptive to other children who were carrying out literacy and numeracy tasks alongside play activities. For example:

> If children are getting too noisy or destructive or they are not playing the correct roles.

> I limit the numbers in there to ensure the play is constructive and not too noisy.

Play as a reward

Studies of reception-class practice (Adams *et al.*, 2004; Fisher, 2001; Bennett *et al.*, 1997) have shown that one of the main ways in which children have access to play is as a reward for completion of adult-intensive tasks. Even when this is not made explicit to children, it is often the case simply because of the way in which play is organised, that is, children work before they play or play until it is their turn to work (play as a holding task). Role-play was also seen not simply as a reward for the completion of formal tasks but also for effort, when 'children had tried hard'. A selection of responses is given below:

> Those who have finished a written or maths assignment generally.

> Children who have worked well. Children who have finished [their] work.

> Free choice when set tasks have been finished.

> Rota and occasionally as a reward.

> Reward, e.g. for finishing [work].

Future agendas

In terms of the future development of role-play in their classrooms, 15 per cent of respondents stated that they would like more time to plan for and subsequently develop role-play in their classrooms. More adults to support children's role-play was also identified as an aim for the future. A few respondents said they would also appreciate more ideas on how to 'do' role-play. Some useful insights were also offered when thinking about how to develop role-play further:

> More courage to let play be more than an add-on extra.

> Spend more time developing children's ideas. (Time is limited in a Key Stage 1 class.)

> The role-play is a very important part of the class. We are always looking for ways to develop and support the children at play and to make each 'setting' stimulating in a variety of ways.

Moving from quantitative to qualitative understandings of teacher perspectives of role-play

Against the background of the questionnaire and pilot work undertaken in a number of reception classes in the two local authorities, we established a sample of three project schools for more detailed study. Our teachers were strongly committed to role-play and expressed an interest in developing it further within their pedagogy. Moreover, the schools reflected the diversity of provision available in the area. Early childhood education in the region is provided mainly by pre-school playgroups and private nurseries. Although the landscape of provision is changing nationally as we write, there were very few state-funded nursery places available at the time. Most children entered reception classes at four, typically in two intakes across the year. Even where nursery provision is more widely available, parents increasingly opt for their children to enter school early for the reasons outlined in Chapter 1. Early entry to primary school meets both the needs of parents and children for free early education, and the schools' need to maintain numbers on rolls (Daniels *et al.*, 1995).

Clearly, the continued practice of admitting four-year-olds to school has had implications for the development of pedagogy in reception classes. On the one hand, it is recognised that young children need opportunities for play and active learning and, on the other, there is an implicit expectation that they are also preparing for formal education. Project classrooms reflected this double-edged pedagogy in how they were organised and resourced. Remembering that the research was undertaken several years after the introduction of the Foundation Stage, we might have expected the classrooms to look more like other early childhood settings, such as nursery classes, and less like primary school classrooms. Although our teachers made generous material provision for play, both indoors and outdoors, their classrooms also included many tables and chairs for teacher-initiated group work. Role-play areas, such as home corners and shops, tended to be set apart from the main stream of classroom activity, in the corners of classrooms, and were usually bounded by screens or drapes. Resources were often elaborate, accessible and attractive to children.

Our teachers worked within the *Curriculum for Guidance Foundation Stage*. This requires practitioners to 'make good use of outdoor space so that children are enabled to learn by working on a larger, more active scale than is possible indoors' (QCA, 2000: 15). Moreover, it acknowledges that 'children learn in different ways and at different rates' and that 'some children will learn more readily outdoors' (2001: 21). With this in mind, two classrooms had developed direct 'free-flow' access to an outdoor space, although in one of these the outdoor area was a playground shared with the rest of the school, which inevitably restricted its use. In the third school an outdoor play area had been developed specifically for reception children but the lack of direct access from the classroom required the teacher to timetable specific sessions for outdoor play, which she did as often as was possible. Our teachers talked to us in interviews, group meetings and also in informal conversations about how they approached role-play. Over the course of the school year six teachers and six teaching assistants participated in the study.

Role-play is based on children's ideas

All of our teachers talked enthusiastically about how highly they valued the contribution role-play makes to young children's emergent ideas about the world on entry to school, and how this aided them in their learning across the curriculum and more widely in relation to lifelong learning. Importantly, however, for role-play to be meaningful to the children, the ideas had to develop from their own interests. As one teacher explained to us '[role-play] is important but it has to come from [the children]. Unless they choose it is not going to be so good'. Broadly speaking, the teachers shared an underlying philosophy that could be described as child-centred, meeting children's needs and learning through play and discovery. In this way, they align with other early childhood and primary teachers whose beliefs have been documented in recent research (Woods *et al.*, 1999; Bennett *et al.*, 1997). However, these ideas were not, as is suggested by some critics of child-centred ideologies, focused solely on the individual child. Indeed, the social dimension of play in which children negotiated collective ideas was at the centre of their thinking about play. Although children's ideas lay at the heart of role-play, our teachers also believed that children need guidance and input from adults. The teacher quoted above explained: 'It's mostly the children's ideas. If we do find that we're getting a bit stuck ... we might suggest and let them take it from there'. In this way, the teachers viewed their role as being responsive to children's play as it developed and they were not against intervening to help children's ideas develop.

Learning through role-play

Role-play has been described as an integrating mechanism in which children can exercise a range of skills and capacities (Bruce, 1996; Wood and Attfield, 2005). We asked the teachers to outline the main purpose of role-play in the early childhood curriculum. They expressed the view that it involves multiple skills, talking about learning through role-play in general terms. However, all of the teachers identified social learning as the most important element. One teacher explained her approach thus:

> Social interaction, I think that's very important for young children. I think it's something that can sort of give real opportunities for children to have free flow playing in that they can go into a situation, they can make a decision, they can decide who they want to be, who they want to play with ... It gives them a chance to take ideas that they see other children do or perhaps they've seen at home or in the classroom and experiment with those ideas really, and know that they're not going to be told that it's right or it's wrong. They've got that freedom to take it how they want to.

In a similar way, a teacher in a different school explained that she prioritised children's language and social development:

> I think probably for me it's the use of language [and] the opportunities for them to talk and explore language for themselves ... also the social side of things ... they have to know about sharing equipment and taking turns and when it's their time to go in there [the role-play area].

This teacher said that she believed role-play gave the children 'a chance to use real experiences, more real, not sort of "out of world" play. It's an opportunity for them to use prior knowledge; it's safe play really'.

Though there were few references to the learning of subjects in the teachers' accounts, one teacher made clear links to the curriculum, especially in the areas of literacy and maths: '[We] need to try make sure there's an opportunity for writing which we might start off but then the children will come up to us and say oh we need this ... we want to write a list.'

The emphasis on children's ideas and 'freedom to pursue their own agenda', prevalent in all teachers' accounts, clearly had implications for how they approached planning and also for how they viewed their role in the children's play. In two of the three classrooms, children's ideas were nested within agreed topics, which in turn were determined by the school's agreed programme. Within this overarching framework, teachers chose a theme or focus for the role-play area:

> The sort of 'umbrella' idea ... comes from the rolling programme for the school, so the classroom assistant and I will choose a theme which we think the children will be interested in and is kind of related to the school theme. If it's a theme that's very wide, or you know perhaps [there] might be aspects of it that aren't good to grab in children, then we might tweak it. So we're thinking of three role-play themes for the term that last a few weeks each.

In the second school the teachers also worked within long-term plans established at the start of the year:

> [We] follow our long term plan. We have a look at the different topic – we don't call it that – but then we think OK, what might be role-play areas for that, so we just come up with a few ideas of our own. But we are then child-led so that when the children start school we have a discussion with them and say this is what we're going to do this term or half term ... so what could we have in the classroom that you could play [with].

There were occasional tensions between teachers' and children's perspectives on the value of a particular theme. On one occasion a teacher had set up a stimulating role-play area related to other classroom work. It subsequently became very popular with the children and led to some episodes of highly imaginative play. However, after a few days the teacher deemed it to be 'unsuccessful', stating 'I had reservations about this and it's just not working – they don't know what to do in here and the quality of the play is not good enough'. The teacher decided to change the role-play area into something else. It is easy for adults to base a decision on a snapshot of children's activity. Observation, described as a 'luxury' by one of our teachers, might have seen the rich and imaginative examples of play. As adults we bring our own notions of 'quality' and these are in turn wrapped up in adult perceptions of educational discourses and agendas. These are important too. But the children's perspective of what is and is not successful in play may be at odds with these. In the week following the teacher's decision to change the role-play area, Fred asked the teacher why their role-play theme had been removed because he had really liked playing in there. As we will see in more detail in Chapter 5, even when children offer resistance or articulate their concerns, they are often unable to affect the outcome of adult decisions in educational environments.

Wider influences

One of the teachers adopted a very different approach to role-play, in that she had no rolling programme or long-term plan. Rather she thought in terms of project work, inspired by a recent visit to the pre-schools of Reggio Emilia. Her starting point was listening to the children's conversations and observing their persistent interests in the first weeks of the school term. She explained that role-play areas were based on:

> Discussions with the children. I might offer up ideas but ultimately it is the children that decide. It is basically their decision, if they didn't want something we just wouldn't have it. It really is about what they are interested in, [it] would be down to the children and within reason I try to accommodate their needs and ideas in the projects that we develop.

This approach to working with the children could be described as a negotiated or co-constructed pedagogy. Rather than see herself as the teacher-in-charge she relinquished some of her control in order to listen to the children and genuinely draw their ideas into her approach. At one point in her interview she talked about how her practice had changed:

> When I went to Reggio it 'blew my mind really' and I was able to look at other ways of teaching/learning and good practice. I'm not here to be the best teacher I'm here to help [the children] get what they can out of it. They need to be more in control of their learning, this is their place [so] what do they want to get out of it? If you give them the responsibility they can deal with it. Ultimately I could have the final say but I say to them: this is your classroom but I work here as well so between us we need to agree. Everything here gets discussed and talked about.

Clearly, this teacher believed that while it was possible to plan for specific outcomes in structured play activities, this was not the case in children's free play. Her views are similar to those of a teacher reported in an earlier study of teachers' theories who coined the phrase 'planning for possibilities' (Bennett et al., 1997). By this she meant that the teacher can provide an environment that is suggestive rather than prescriptive, thus allowing children to create their own contexts, plots and narratives. This phrase also captures the tensions that are inherent in planning for an activity that is essentially about the intentions of the player, the social dynamic and interactions between groups of players. Does the curriculum impact on role-play in, for example, time, resources, literacy/numeracy? Yes it does, but the planning guidelines do talk about offering opportunities for role-play. And it is not always about resources – it just needs initiative and autonomy on the children's behalf. Role-play is good for literacy, as it encourages speaking and listening, children have to learn to negotiate roles, and most of all it is good for language development.

For this teacher 'there are loads of opportunities, both planned and unplanned ... Role-play can be a focus for teaching or it can be a completely free activity'.

Though there were some differences between the starting points for planning role-play areas, our teachers agreed that planning for role-play was not the same as planning for other activities. Their main skill was to provide the appropriate resources and environment. One teacher described how her children had 'the freedom to pursue their own agenda ... within the group dynamic. It's that freedom and the experimentation that they are able to do ... that they might not necessarily be allowed to do elsewhere'.

Intervening in role-play

There is little agreement in the literature about how much or how little teachers should direct role-play, although recent literature on the subject has moved towards one of greater participation and reciprocity between teachers and children. Research has also consistently shown that early childhood teachers do not, as a rule, involve themselves in children's role-play, but there is little in the literature to determine why this is the case. Kitson argues that 'effective intervention can channel ... learning, helping children to construct new dilemmas and challenges, encouraging and supporting individuals and extending and motivating language performance and competence' (1997: 112). We have used the term teacher deliberately here rather that the more general term 'adult' since it connotes a particular set of roles and responsibilities in the school context and highlights the tension that appears to exist between teachers teaching on the one hand, and children playing on the other (Bennett and Kell, 1989). That is not to say that the many other adults who worked in the project classrooms did not have a part to play in supporting and managing children's role-play.

We observed that teachers were usually engaged in other activities while children role-played. In this way their practice reflected earlier studies of play in reception classes where role-play functioned as a 'holding task', recreation or reward for children while teachers attended to other tasks (Bennett and Kell, 1989; Bennett et al., 1997; Adams et al., 2004). Our teachers' approach to intervention in role-play can be organised under the following headings:

- getting children started/giving them ideas;
- helping children to resolve conflict;
- preventing disruptive behaviour;
- extending learning;
- by invitation.

Elsewhere it has been argued that child-centred methodology denies the teacher 'a full role in the most demanding aspect of assisting in a child's education, that of operating at a high level of skill as a teacher' (Meadows and Cashdan, 1988: 4). In other words, teachers are positioned beyond the boundaries of the child's world, their passive orientation contrasted with the child's active one (Walkerdine, 1986). However, there were more pragmatic reasons for not being more involved in play, as this teacher explained:

> Now of course again the theory is that a practitioner should be able to go around and observe all these things. But you can't because you're stuck with your teaching group and that's why we like the play board because at least it can give us ... not the total quality of what the play was like but at least it tells us who's visited what and it would just be a luxury just to have time to do observations like that, but to be honest it doesn't really happen in the mornings, it happens in the afternoons, again because we haven't got the constraints of tasks ... I'd like to think I'd only intervene if I thought that there was a problem with sharing ... or [if] one child was being upset by another, some sort of policing I suppose. And that happens more inside than outside because of noise levels because of space etc. But ... I wouldn't say it happened much outside at all, only if, you know, there's ... children playing with ... if there's an oar going to snap over someone's head that sort of thing ... I just like them to take to play as they want really.

It was noted earlier that all teachers believed that role-play was derived predominantly from the children's own ideas negotiated in a social context. Equally, however, they recognised that children sometimes needed help from adults:

> Sometimes you need to give them ideas otherwise the play becomes stagnant, they don't always have the 'ideas' to move it on so sometimes you have to suggest certain things.

> We do sometimes ... we get dragged into it which is quite lovely ... they come out with a phone and say there's so and so on the phone ... We will sometimes intervene if it's for a literacy session and say we notice that they're sitting there looking at each other thinking [we're] not really sure, so I might go in and start something off, but I quickly withdraw out of that.

Scaffolding play through skilled intervention

On many occasions during our visits the children, particularly the boys, engaged in boisterous physical play, such as running, chasing and rolling, in their role-play. We observed this kind of play behaviour in all three classrooms as part of children's role-play. However, not surprisingly such activity was necessarily quickly curtailed by the adults: few classrooms can accommodate easily this type of play. At times children's role-play clearly exceeded the boundaries of what was deemed acceptable behaviour in school, such was its exuberant and active nature. What constitutes 'acceptable' play in the classroom? This issue is not easily resolved either conceptually or practically. The project teachers recognised that role-play is by its very nature often noisy and physical. Yet at the same time such play presented teachers with a problem regarding both its educational value and its potentially disruptive influence on classroom life. It was clear that noisy and physical role-play could not easily be sanctioned in project classrooms and compelled adults to intervene. The range of interventions, however, in such instances varied from those that terminated the play altogether to those that attempted to work with the play. In one instance, the children were getting very noisy in the role-play area and on three occasions the teacher had intervened finally saying, 'I didn't say go in there and make as much noise as you'd like! I think you get very excited in there and your voices get too loud!' On a different occasion the noise level became so great that the play was 'spilling over' into the adjacent work area. The teacher came into the 'café' and took the role of the customer:

Teacher: Are you open?
Greg: Yes.
Teacher: Have you got a menu in your café?
(One of the boys hands the teacher a menu.)
Teacher: What flavour soups have you got?
Greg: Mint.
Teacher: Mint, what other soup have you got?
Greg: Tomato.
Teacher: Have you got oxtail soup?
Freddie: Yeah.
Teacher: Right I'll have that then with a bread roll and butter.
(Robbie comes in and asks Miss Smith if he can come in to the café.)
Teacher: You'll have to ask the others, I'm not Miss Smith, I'm Amy today.

The second example clearly illustrates how the teacher skilfully directs the play back by becoming the 'customer' and entering into the role-play rather than adopting a regulatory or adult-imposed sanction. This teacher reflected on how they sometimes have to intervene but how they might do that productively:

> So we do have to intervene ... but then again we try not to go into the middle of the game or the play and say right okay it's, it's a bit loud, we try and take on a role so we'll knock at the door and salute the guard and try and get round it in that way. [We] try not to say 'ooh it's too noisy, can you

please quieten down' but, you know, have you had a party? And just by talking about it ... the noise level was brought down and I could go out again.

Grouping children for role-play

Grouping is a common and necessary strategy for organising children for particular learning experiences in the school context (Blatchford et al., 2003). Children may be grouped by their ability to undertake a task, the nature of a task itself or they may be able to self-select groupings on the basis of friendships. There are potential problems in each approach unless carefully monitored. When the teacher allows children to select whom they work or play with, social divisions may be reinforced (e.g. on the basis of gender and ability), thereby isolating those children who are not chosen (Blatchford et al., 2003: 166). Paley (1992) introduced the rule 'you can't say you can't play' to overcome children's exclusion of one another. At the same time if children are placed in groups by their teachers then group dynamics may prevent some children from participating fully in a task or may lead to their adopting stereotypical roles; for example, in a mixed gender group, girls may adopt the role of secretary or scribe while the boys solve problems. Similarly, a child whose first language is not the dominant language may be excluded from full participation in the activity.

In play activities, children will tend to select same-gender partners and friends. This is not surprising as most studies have found little difference in the number of friends that boys and girls have but there is strong evidence that they do associate with the same sex (Thorne, 1993). Same-sex friend selection is more common in early childhood settings than in the home, where more mixed gender play is observed (Dunn, 2004). In the project classrooms we observed different approaches to grouping in each of the classrooms at different times:

> I used to group them but now I see it as a fairly negative process. Grouping is more about the management of the curriculum and doesn't really serve any purpose [and can lead to] negative labelling which can create disaffection. I might say 'we need four people in the pet-shop and two on the computers' but I don't group them.

This teacher also allowed children to group themselves in their free play time while others worked within teacher-selected groups:

> I don't group them ... it's pretty much self selecting but for example on a morning where the key areas are English and maths, Debbie or I or Ruth would be working with a focus, then the other children are free to choose the whole range of activities in the room so they are self selecting. If they want to go in the role-play they will but obviously [the]

children who Debbie and I are working with ... have to do that specific activity and [then] they all swap.

Her approach was also twofold. During focused activities she grouped the children herself and at 'planning time' children negotiated their own groups:

> We do when we use [the role-play areas] for the literacy activities that we do, so it might be that we send a particular group in there to go in and work on a story and come back and act it out for us or just to go and have some more play time. But when they have their planning time that's their free choice so the children that end up in there are the ones that have done the deal with whoever when they've been sitting on the carpet ...

It was reported in Bennett *et al.* (1997) that teachers also engineer play groups as a way to support those children who lack the skills or the confidence to play. Of the three settings, one catered for a small number of children with English as a second language: 'We do sometimes put children in [the role-play area] if we think there are a couple of children, if maybe their language skills aren't [strong] we sometimes match them up with that specific purpose'.

   Whatever grouping strategy is adopted it is clear that vigilance on the part of teachers is required to ensure that it is an inclusive and positive experience for all children.

Challenges and constraints

In the interviews and project group meetings with the teachers, we reflected on the structural issues that directly and indirectly regulate children's behaviour and, moreover, on how we might be able to understand the issues from the children's perspective. One teacher explained that in her classroom a major inhibiting factor in developing role-play was simply lack of space, particularly as the number of children increased:

> There are constraints of time and space. That's going to be a really big issue next term when we've got thirty children in that small space and I'm really worried ... and concerned about how we're going to do that. It's always time and space ... we're hoping to get round that next term by trying to have groups outside in the outside play area all day if we can but that's just dependent on the weather.

This teacher also talked about how in her school they were addressing the issue of space and its negative effects on the quality of children's role-play. Developing the outdoor area had been seen as a means of reducing the need to contain children in ways that were often detrimental to the play:

We now have our outside area as well so that's moved some of the space issue and the noise kind of thing that might occur ... so that it isn't such a constraint that it may have been a year ago ... extending role-play to the 'outside' is the next step. We do use outside now when we can get out there but it would be nice to have what others are developing in their area. It's the logistics of it all at the moment ... there's a sand-tray, bikes and big blocks but they are scattered all over the school so I would love to get a shed where we can store it all. If the classroom assistant is away, forget it because you just can't do it on your own, getting it all out, packing it all away. The bigger space outside means they won't be as constrained as they inevitably are inside the classroom.

A strategy used by all project teachers to manage children in the role-play areas was to limit the number of children who were able to use the indoor role-play area to a maximum of four or five children at a time. Interestingly, the teachers rarely needed to reinforce this rule, so embedded was it in the classroom cultures. The 'numbers rule' was a management strategy introduced by adults, but imposed by the children to restrict access to the role-play area. It functioned, albeit indirectly, as a pedagogical tool to manage and control role-play. In this sense classroom rules are forms of intervention even when they are not applied explicitly. We will say more about the 'numbers rule' in Chapter 5 since it was used by the children in a range of ways and not simply in the ways the teachers had originally intended.

As we saw with the quantitative data earlier, particularly in mixed class settings, the impact of the curriculum affects the time and space available for role-play, as one teacher illustrates:

Well I know the theory is that when children are engaged in free flow play [they should] take it on and develop it until it comes to a natural end, but the practicalities are that, certainly [in] the mixed age class the expectation is that we teach literacy and mathematics and that you have a break time, so for example the children might be involved in some really good quality play and its quarter past ten you need to do the plenary, I need to get them outside so that I can change my activities from mathematics-based to English-based and I have got to have them outside so that I can do it, so regardless what the quality of the play is they have to go outside so that I can do it. I feel now the profile has been raised again through the foundation stage, but it's almost like it's come a bit too late because everyone's so squashed by maths and English but you know the foundation stage should have come first ... but now I think people are too worried and too entrenched in and worried about meeting targets and things.

This teacher also raised the point about the 'progression' of the reception children into Year 1 and what lies ahead for them:

> I think as we get to the end of Reception ... you're conscious that they're going into Year One and things are going to be a bit different ... I think towards the end of the year maybe we're a little bit conscious that [there is] less time for play ...

Teachers' perspectives on gender

Our teachers were fully aware of promoting positive images of gender and culture but there was less evidence of the social challenging of stereotypes in practice (see also Woods *et al.*, 1999). Moreover, research over the past few decades has highlighted how education largely reflects the broader societal gendered power relationships (Robinson and Jones Diáz, 2006). One teacher suggested that 'children come to school with perceptions of what they should be doing as a gender type', implying that 'it is beyond the power of the school to prevent children seeking a definition of gender-appropriate behaviour' (Jordan, 1995: 73). The teachers were exercised by the types of stereotypical roles children chose and in response created role-play areas that they hoped would have wider appeal and were less gender distinct, for example, a castle, a pirate ship and a spaceship. Although the teachers attempted to 'de-gender' role-play provision through differing themes, many children continued to pursue largely their own agendas: children do not learn uncritically, nor adopt passively educators' attempts to offer less gendered role-play ideas (Browne and Ross, 1991). Struck by the amount of gender-stereotypical play, we were interested to explore with the teachers their perspectives on gendered play, and how they accommodate the individual needs of the child as well as widening children's gender scripts to open up other (role) play possibilities.

Teachers were asked if they felt there were differences for girls and boys in terms of what they chose to play and whether they felt they should intervene in terms of stereotypical play:

Teacher: I can see that in the classroom ... with some children who really like the dolls and want to play with the dolls and ... very rarely touch a block or piece of construction equipment. By the same token there are boys who would never dream of touching a doll. They are really happy to be working with construction ...

Researcher: Do you think you have a responsibility or a role to challenge that or not?

Teacher: I think as a practitioner I think that you can offer them the opportunity of seeing that it's all right to step out of that perception. But I don't think you can force the issue but it could cause too [many] problems it could cause too much angst it might do. But I think it's right that those children should be offered the opportunity of seeing girls and boys stepping into other non-stereotypical roles really but I don't think you can do any more than offer them the opportunity. Boys tend to engage in 'superhero' discourse and run around as opposed to the girls who tend to keep it quite neat.

Also in some settings, because the researchers were often literally inside the role-play settings and with the children for sustained periods of time, the stereotypical elements of their narratives were more prevalent than they may have been for teachers who may be observing from a distance whilst undertaking other activities. For example, this teacher says:

If you had asked me that last year I'd have said yes, quite likely that the boys will take on boy-type, you know, stereotypical roles and this year we've found they haven't done that. So the boys have become queens or little Red Riding Hood ... because we've gone 'oh hi, Miss Riding Hood' and not paid any attention to whether it's male or female, maybe they feel a bit safer ...

Conclusion

Clearly there is no one way to plan an environment that supports children's imaginative role-play activity. Much will depend on the type of setting, resources and space available, and the ethos of the early childhood practitioners. Most importantly, the environment should also be developed in response to the needs of a particular group of children in terms of their age, maturity, cultural and linguistic background, the nature of the surrounding community and the things that really interest them. In spite of differences in the pedagogical practices of the project teachers, all shared the belief that role-play had an important part to play in young children's learning. Perhaps most interesting of all is the way that the project teachers felt similarly constrained to the teachers who responded to the questionnaire. This was in spite of the major changes to curriculum policy that ought to have made it easier for reception-class teachers to resolve the tensions that clearly exist between the aims of an early childhood curriculum and the aims of the primary school. Policy is one thing, but implementation and realisation of policy is, quite clearly, another.

Having identified how the teachers planned for role-play and their underpinning philosophies about the role of play in the Foundation Stage, we turn now, in the following two chapters, to the children's perspectives and how they 'received' the role-play that the teachers provided for them.

Chapter 5

Exploring role-play from the children's perspective

I don't like the spaceship 'cos I love that [pointing to the travel agency]. I don't like the phones, supposed to be pretend but it ain't got no batteries in there. You can't ring real people up it's just pretend.

(Zac, aged 4)

Nothing's real it's playing a game.

(Lucy, aged 4)

Having established in the preceding chapters that role play appears to be the preferred form of social engagement and play for children aged three to five, and that our teachers believed that it is a vital activity in the early childhood curriculum, we turn our attention in this chapter to the children's views on the matter. The above extracts illustrate vividly that young children have strong views about the activities offered to them in school. The extracts also reveal some aspects of the complexity of role-play, most notably the distinction between what is real and what is not real. We might not be surprised at Zac's appreciation that 'it's just pretend' and Lucy's explanation of the distinction between real and pretend. These brief extracts nevertheless point to two central themes. First, as we endeavoured to explain in Chapter 2, recognition of alternative realities is a remarkable feat of human achievement and, to recall Harris (2000), lays the foundations for many other skills in later life. More than that, and this brings us to our second point, children like pretending. They enjoy the experience and tangible 'feeling' of being something or someone other than themselves. Indeed, the actual experience of pretending is something that we might all recall. What also became clear is that if the act of pretending is in the company of friends, then, children told us, better still. The pleasure associated with role-play is noted also by Dunn (2004) in her extensive and seminal work on the emergence of friendship in young children. Here she notes that 'pretence can lead to particular emotions – excitement, fear, amusement ... the pleasure of generating such emotions together with another child is very clear' (29).

As we have emphasised throughout the book, the children's perspectives of role-play lie at the heart of the project. We believed firmly in the children's capacity to share their unique insights and knowledge with us, so that we might gain a deeper understanding of particular aspects of their role-play from the 'inside'. The challenge for us in this chapter is to retain something of the integrity of the children's perspectives and to represent them as fairly as possible. However, we take the view that we are acting on behalf of children, reporting as fully as possible their often unarticulated efforts to make sense of experiences that are, for the most part, controlled in some way or another by adults. With this in mind, we focus in this chapter on children's definitions of role-play, what they liked and didn't like, their favourite themes and the strategies they adopted to fulfil their desire to play in particular places and with particular friends.

Children talking about role-play

We established a relationship with the children through our initial visits and participation in the routines of the classrooms and on this basis we developed methods that would both be familiar to the children and take place within the context of their classrooms and normal daily routine. We had explained to the children already that they were part of a play project and that we were interested in their play, and what they liked and didn't like about it. In addition, many of the children had chosen special play project names. To explore the concept of role-play, its place in school and what children liked and didn't like about it, we invited the children to negotiate their own small groups, a strategy that we believed would be supportive to children and enable them to feel confident. To help frame our questions we developed a series of vignettes, for example:

- I like our pretend play area because ...
- Sometimes I do not like pretend play because ...
- New children coming to this school would like our pretend-play areas because ...

These three main questions were embedded in a story based around a visit to their schools from an alien. Stories are, of course, a powerful way to engage children's interest (Baldock, 2006) and to elicit their views about their experiences and what matters to them. The use of stories as a method, particularly those about topics of interest such as 'aliens' and 'new children coming to school', clearly made 'human sense' (Donaldson, 1978) to the children.

What do children like about role-play?

In Chapter 2 we discussed the way in which role-play is characterised by specific forms of language and communication, in particular metacommunicative language, which defines the boundaries of the role-play frame, and signals players' awareness of alternative realities. The children used the language of 'let's pretend' in their play, and spent much time planning, negotiating plots and assigning roles to one another, traits that are highly characteristic of role-play in four- and five-year-olds. The children's comments in response to the question 'what is role-play?' revealed a deep understanding of the distinction between what is real and not real. Many of the children made explicit reference to this distinction as they talked in their groups.

Dan: Doesn't mean it's real, it's just pretend.
Lucy: Nothing's real it's playing a game.
Megan: Pretend play is like something that's not real.
Alex: It means pretend play, doesn't have to be real.
Flower: I can pretend that I can be a unicorn ... not that I am a unicorn but I pretend!
Annie: We play lots of things, sometimes we play mums and dads.
Craig: It's really fun because you can pretend you're a real travel agent.
Ann: [It's] good you can pretend it's real.
Mark: I imagine I'm in a police car.
Siän: ... you can play in it; it's really fun because you can pretend you are a real travel agent.

Studies of play (see Garvey, 1990 for example) suggest that even children under three are able to make this distinction, but may not fully understand or be able to articulate it until they are older. At four years old, the children in the project are able to articulate the distinction between two rather abstract concepts in quite sophisticated ways. The children appear to have an impressive grasp of the very essence of role-play, giving numerous examples from their experiences. However, when we asked the children to tell us *why* there was a role-play area in their classroom, the children gave a rather different perspective. Their comments make little reference to the act of pretence or to the distinction between real and not real. Rather they focused more squarely on learning and specific topics or themes. In the following extract, taken from a group discussion, the children's answers refer to the class topic, and what they have learned. The language used was less elaborate and children did not refer to having fun or to the imaginative content.

Researcher: Why do you think there is a pretend play area [here]?
Jessie: We're learning 'bout 'em. [Pets 'n' Vets]
Popstar: We're learning things in school and then we play in there with them ...
Lewis: We learn about them every week.

This an interesting difference in perception, a separation of definition and function perhaps engendered by the researcher's questions. We are reminded here of the distinction between play in school and play *as such* suggested by Guha (1998), where it is recognised that play in school engages with contexts beyond play as such and this is a central distinction in meaning (Rogers, 2000). Role-play in school is often prescribed by real-world learning and curriculum objectives rather than the interests and inclinations of the children. As Howard *et al.* (2001) suggest, an activity may have the defining characteristics of play, yet according to context the same activity in a new location may take on a different meaning to the player. The project children appeared also to recognise this positioning of role-play in school learning.

During these group discussions, we asked children what they liked and disliked about role-play. First of all, we were struck by the importance they attributed to the experience of being in role or 'pretending' and the obvious pleasure and enjoyment associated with this. The children also talked about how they liked the time to be able to play and to have fun:

> *Jane:* I love it, I love it, 'cos it's got lots of things in it.
> *Joel:* Because it's fun and it's got lots of toys in it.
> *Sara:* I think it was lovely and I pretended to be a rainbow cat with lots of colours.

Not all children, however, enjoyed role-play. For a few, it was an arduous task that they associated with work, particularly when it involved writing.

> *Luke:* I don't like the hard work in there ... all the writing ... some people want to do the writing.
> *Jessie:* I don't like writing in there.
> *Lewis:* I don't like working in there.

These children, although new to school, were already distinguishing clearly between work and play, and identifying some activities as 'hard'. This is unsurprising given the dichotomy between work and play that exists in many educational settings (Bruce, 1991). Other children disliked role-play for social reasons. Richard objected to being excluded by other children, saying, 'I don't like it when the other people don't let you have a go in there'. Nicola had been greatly preoccupied with playing with toy animals. On several occasions she played alone, developing lengthy and complex narratives lasting for as long as forty minutes. After one particularly absorbing bout of pretend play, Nicola rejoined the main group. She announced that 'it was good that Matthew was away today as I got to play with that' (pointing to the animals). Our observations showed that a group of fairly boisterous boys also liked playing with the animals and they would often take over Nicola's space and start playing with the animals. Nicola's response to the boys' intervention was usually to relinquish the animals and leave the play. Some time later in a group discussion, Nicola explained why she no longer liked the animal play. Her comment 'it's boring' conceals a deeper concern about the intrusion of the boys.

Nicola:	I just don't go in there very much, I do other things.
Louise:	Play with animals?
Nicola:	Not anymore!
Researcher:	Why is that?
Nicola:	All the boys just kept playing and taking the animals.
Nicola:	It's boring!
Researcher:	Why is it boring?
Nicola:	Not really boring but a little bit boring, some stuff just plastic and some stuff metal.
Sarah:	No, I like it.

Being with friends

We have seen how role-play can be difficult and socially challenging, particularly if the children feel powerless to challenge their peers as in Nicola's case. Nevertheless, one of the most significant themes to emerge from the children's data was the value they placed upon role-play as a vehicle to be with their friends. In the course of the project, many children identified special friends in the class and used role-play explicitly as a way of being with them:

Researcher:	Who did you choose, Katy, to play in the Travel Agency today?
Katy:	I chose Mia, Roxy and Peter. I didn't choose Sam, Peter choosed him 'cos that's his friend.
Researcher:	Why did you choose Mia and Roxy?
Katy:	Because they're my friends.

Grant has chosen Tony and Marcus because, he says: 'they are my best friends'.

Researcher:	Do you like going into the role-play area with your best friends?
Grant:	Yes.
Researcher:	Do you get to choose often?
Grant:	Not really, not very often.

Playing with friends and best friends was important to the children and was central to why they chose role-play over other activities:

Sarah: I play with Ann and Madeline [in there] because they're my friends.
Charlie: I like playing in there with David ... he's my friend.

Jenna: I played with Lizzie and Ellis in there, I played games.
Researcher: What games did you play?
Jenna: Mummy, daddy and sisters, I was a mummy.
Researcher: Why do you like playing that?
Jenna: Because we can be friends.

Within the school environment, grouping children for play and hence access to friends is often controlled by adults. In the project, the adults' approach to grouping children sometimes ran counter to children's preferred choice of playmates. However, where children had choice they were adept at engineering situations to ensure they could play with their friends. Many children were observed making 'pacts' with each other so that if they were chosen they would then choose their friend. Often if children were negotiating with other children or trying to persuade others to play with them they would say 'I'll be your friend' as leverage to get the desired outcome. For example, Lucy tried to persuade Alice to be the patient by saying, 'I'll be your best friend'. Alice returned and Lucy said to her, 'Come on get into bed! I'll be your best friend ... you won't come to my party' [further leverage]. Alice agreed to be the patient but then asked to go to the toilet. When Alice came back she said: 'I'm going to a party today anyway'.

In the following example two boys, Liam and Max, start fighting over the money box. In order to win the box Liam uses 'friendship' as the 'trump' card:

Liam: I want that!
Max: No, you can't have it, I want it!
Liam: I won't be your friend!
Max: All right then. (*Passes the box to Liam. Liam takes the box, lowers his head and smiles to himself. He realises he has won.*)

Liam, one of the younger children in the class, knows what he needs to say to achieve his desired outcome. His smile of self-satisfaction at the end of the encounter when he finally has the money box in his hands revealed all.

Children quickly learned on entry to school how social networks operated within the classroom. Steven (aged four) had been in school for just a few weeks. At 'choosing time' (i.e. when one child is chosen by the teacher to be the 'special helper' and that child can then choose other children to help them with particular tasks or activities), he watched Tony closely while he chose another child in the class to help him. Tony took a while to choose but eventually chose Martin to help him. Steven said:

Steven: I knew he would choose Martin.
Joe: How did you know that, Steven?
Steven: I knewed he would choose him 'cos he's Tony's friend.

Children's desire to affiliate with others and maintain friendships often took precedence over the content and nature of the play. For example, on one occasion three girl friends tried to enter the role-play area together. The children playing in there told them that they could not come in as there were already too many children (the class teacher operates a 'four only' rule). Rhiannon (one of the children trying to enter the role-play), asked the classroom assistant to assist in negotiating access but her request was refused. Rather than be separated from one another all three girls left the role-play area and moved into an adjacent room and proceeded to draw pictures and talk. On this occasion they abandoned the role-play to preserve the friendship group.

Young children (like adults) want the emotional well-being and stability that friends can provide. Moreover, they are building the concept of friendship and do not separate friendship from their daily activities (Broadhead, 2004). They also learn from early schooling that interaction with peers is fragile and acceptance can sometimes be difficult (Corsaro, 1997). Friendship formation is therefore important in children's social, cognitive and affective development, acquisition of their interpersonal skills, and their later adjustment to social life (Avgitidou, 1997). Moreover, sophisticated qualities of friendship such as intimacy, proximity, self-disclosure and sharing, normally associated with older children and adults, are in fact evident in the relationships formed by very young children (Dunn, 2004; Corsaro, 1985). Role-play, then, can provide an ideal context for the development of social skills that for young children in particular evolve within such contexts as the formation and termination of friendships. The ways in which play is organised in school will, therefore, influence the nature of children's friendships and opportunities for socialisation. Several studies consider specifically the impact of classroom practices on children's social development (Corsaro, 1985; Avgitidou, 1997; McLean, 1994; Trawick-Smith, 1998), and suggest that over-prescriptive and highly structured environments militate against the kind of peer-group activity that would lead to the development of social skills in the context of children's friendships.

As Corsaro also observed, children often try to develop friendships with several playmates to ensure successful entry to groups or activities and, ultimately, to satisfy peer interaction. Sometimes the children appeared unsure about who counted as friends and sought confirmation and reassurance on the context of role-play. For example, Lauren approaches Carl and asks, 'You like me, don't you?' This was an interesting exchange because Lauren is one of the older children in the class and seemed on the surface to be very confident, often taking on an authority role, and directing the play. However, asking Carl that question suggests an underlying anxiety as to whether she was liked by other children in the group at that time. This aligns with Dunn (2004) who suggests that 'talk with friends about mental states is most common in joint pretend play and understanding psychological states is revealed and fostered in such settings' (94).

Role-play also provided opportunities for children to reflect on friendships (and role-play) with children in their pre-school environments:

Ria: You were at Butterflies pre-school. It was really fun at pre-school I liked it there.
Matt: Yeah 'cos you get to play there all the time.
Ria: You still did work but not like it is here.
Jenni: Charlie, do you remember when we were in pre-school, Ali was the mum, you was the dad and I was the daughter.

From the children's perspectives, developing and sustaining a shared imaginary world and friendship are closely linked: 'the pretend play that develops with friends is more sustained, more complex, and more harmonious' (Dunn, 2004: 29). The acquisition of social and communication skills is vital in the process of early learning and central to the early all-round development of young children at a time when they are both motivated by, and highly receptive to, peer-group activity and the development and maintenance of friendships (Corsaro, 1985). Moreover, peer culture has been described as an essential part of the formation of children as schoolboys and schoolgirls and ultimately could be related to how productive the school experience is for children (Maclean, 1996). This is perhaps unsurprising given that role-play is, by its very nature, a social and intersubjective experience. Throughout the project, role-play occupied a central place in the peer culture of each classroom, enabling the children to create shared meanings, and form and re-form alliances with one another.

Playing the game?

One of the central aims of this project was to examine how the children responded to role-play provision and classroom pedagogy. Within classroom pedagogy, children are often 'powerless' on two counts: first, they are pupils under educational supervision and authority and, second, they are children to the adults around them. They may also be powerless in their relationships with other children on account of their gender, race, ability and personal characteristics. We observed children in all three situations of powerlessness, yet in many instances they made concerted efforts to gain control over the direction of their role-play and, far from being passive recipients of the demands meted out to them by others, they actively engaged strategies to reconstruct and reinvent the parameters of the activity, even when their actions contradicted or challenged the class routines and expectations of adults. Indeed, we observed children engaged in acts of outright resistance or in strategies that actively challenged classroom pedagogy. We conceptualise these strategies as 'playing the game' since the spontaneous and unsanctioned responses were often integral and necessary to the success of their play. The strategies adopted by children within role-play resonate with similar concepts of 'secondary adjustment to school rules' and 'working the system' identified by Goffman and documented in Corsaro's work on pre-school peer culture (1997, 2005). Corsaro notes: 'children's secondary adjustments in preschool settings contribute to group identity and provide children with a tool for addressing personal interests and goals' (1997: 133). In the same way for our children, 'playing the game' was integral to preserving peer culture within play, to finding ways to realise play interests and goals, and was for the children a way of sustaining and developing their role-play in the face of adult interests and goals.

Coping with interruptions

When children were engaged in role-play, the teachers and teaching assistants were usually engaged in adult-intensive activities. The point was made in Chapter 4 that current ways of working in many reception classes mean that teachers are juggling several different priorities at the same time in order to meet the perceived requirements of the curriculum, and that it is possible to argue that play becomes a holding task, even when it is also valued highly by adults as a child-initiated peer-group activity. In all three classrooms, children were routinely pulled away from role-play by adults to undertake other tasks. These interruptions, to hear readers, change books or give additional help to children with perceived special needs, were often a source of frustration and even subversion for children. Such was the determination of some children to complete a game or pursue a friendship in their role-play that they were prepared to resist and risk conflict with adults. This might involve modifying the classroom environment, and negotiating creative alternatives to adult requests.

It is not our intention to be unduly critical of the teachers, with whom we discussed this issue fully and frankly. Rather we are highlighting, once again, that the ways in which early childhood settings are typically organised, and the multiple demands to provide a wide range of play activities alongside more formal activities particularly in literacy, place huge demands on teachers and, at the same time, prevent children from developing sustained periods of role-play. We argue here that these interruptions were the single most disruptive factor on the quality and length of children's role-play episodes we observed, both indoors and outdoors, for two reasons. First, children clearly needed time to negotiate and assign roles and develop their ideas. Second, the social groups that formed within the play, indeed on which the play some-times depended, were almost always terminated as a result of the adult's interruption. Interrupting play in this way sends out a message to the chil-dren about the 'value' of role-play and may well add to the 'muddled and distorted thinking about play and its meanings' in the classroom (Hall and Abbott, 1991: 30 cited in Keating et al., 2002).

Balanced compliance

To cope with these interruptions, the children adopted a range of different strategies. The first type of strategy we call balanced compliance: balancing their own needs (wanting to be part of the play) with complying with adult requests to leave the play to undertake other tasks. These include stalling and moving boundaries. The second strategy is resistance, which included acts of refusal and subversion.

In the following example, Millie is completely immersed in outdoor 'den play' when the teaching assistant calls her away to read. Millie adopts a 'stalling' technique, and shouts out: 'Take Rosie first!' Rosie is another child in the class who Millie knows also has additional help with reading. The teaching assistant replied: 'Rosie has already been'. Millie pleads with the teaching assistant to be allowed to continue with her play, who tries to cajole her by say-ing that she will only be gone for a few minutes and then she can come back to the play. Mille is clearly frustrated and replies with a resigned 'Ohhh ...'

The following extract from Julie's field notes take up the story:

> Millie returns after about fifteen minutes and heads straight for the den, looks for Cheryl in the den, comes out and looks around the play area. As in so many examples Millie's absence meant the play dissipated and the other children she was playing with have moved on to other activities. Millie spots Cheryl playing with the sand and goes over to join her.
>
> (Field notes)

Millie had no choice but to leave the role-play area. But what is interesting about this example is that Millie headed straight back to play with Cheryl but realising she was no longer in the role-play area she sought Cheryl out, rather than trying to continue with the original role-play activity. It would seem that being with her friend was more important than the game. For Millie, the demise of her original game was still in her mind when she returned to the classroom at the end of the outdoor play period. When the teacher asked the children what they had been playing outside Millie said: 'When I was playing outside in the parachute we played mums and dads. When I was asked to read and [then] nobody was in the parachute and Cheryl was in the water'.

In the following example, a group of children are playing in the hospital but cannot find anyone to be the patient. Chris, after some persuasion from Molly, reluctantly agrees to lie down and take on the role of the patient. At the same time he is called away by an adult to 'change his books'. It is clear he does not want to go, so he puts a strategy in place to deal with his absence, attempting to achieve a compromise between his needs and those of the adult. He was reluctant to abandon the play, so whilst reading to the adult, repositioned the barriers that surround the role-play area. This meant that as he was undertaking his reading he was physically still just inside the role-play area. Another child approached the 'hospital' and Chris immediately interjected, 'You can't go in there, 'cos I'm the patient'. This shows Chris maintaining his role in the play by literally keeping one foot in the role-play area whilst the other half of his body is in the classroom. In doing so he is retaining his contact with the role-play while also acceding to the adult agenda of completing his reading task and changing his books. On Chris's return Molly is then called away to undertake another activity and she says to Rhia: 'Don't let anyone in 'cos I've got to go somewhere'. In this brief episode, the role-play was disrupted twice. Not surprisingly, it was difficult for the play to develop in any meaningful and sustained way.

Children also made pacts with each other to ensure that if they were removed from the role-play area their place would not be filled by another child in their absence, what Corsaro (2005: 141) refers to as 'defending interactive space', wanting to continue sharing what they are already sharing, minimise disruption and retain some control over their play activity. For example, Hannah is called away to do her book bag and as she leaves she says to Rhia, 'Don't let anyone else in here'. Eliza arrives in the area and sits down at the computer; as agreed with Hannah, Rhia says: 'Eliza you can't go there 'cos Hannah's playing'. Eliza leaves the area and on this occasion their pact works and Hannah's place is secured for her return.

Resistance

At other times children overtly 'resisted' adult decisions, as the following example recorded in field notes illustrates. The teacher chose four children to go into the role-play area. She told the children that two have to 'work' in the travel shop and the other two children have to be the customers. It was clear that none of the children wanted to take the role of the customer.

Kim says to the teacher, 'Me and Chloe don't want to be in the travel shop'. The teacher says they have to stay in there. Chloe and Kim's resistance is increased and they stand in the shop but will not join in the play. Fifteen minutes later Kim and Chloe are still standing in the shop and will not engage with the role-play. They keep looking to the researcher to rescue the situation but she decides to ignore their non-verbal cues and see how they manage the situation.

Kim starts to join in with a transaction that is taking place in the role-play area and Chloe says to her: 'We're not playing this are we? It's boring!' Kim, having been reprimanded by Chloe, changes tack and says, 'This is a baby's computer, we're five and we want "five" things to do'. Chloe says: 'This is boring!'

This is a very interesting exchange as Kim is one of the most vocal children in the class and Chloe often seemed timid. Yet in this scenario Chloe takes charge and Kim is (re)adjusting her stance to fall in line with Chloe's continued resistance.

Then Lauren enters the shop and Chloe says to her: 'We don't want to be here, it's boring'. Lauren says, 'Well come out then!' but Chloe replies, 'We're not allowed'.

Kim's and Chloe's resistance was not 'heard' or acknowledged by the adults in the classroom, and the two girls were powerless to do anything but withdraw their participation. They each sustained a position of resistance for the entire session. For Chloe and Kim, being coerced into a role that they had declined verbally on several occasions revealed their lack of 'power' in relation to the 'adult authority role' and left them no option but to pursue a path of resistance. Corsaro notes that within peer culture these strategies are 'innovative and collective responses to the adult world' (2005: 93). Children not only identify themselves with a group in the social world of the classroom but also in opposition to other groups, such as adults and in this case also the younger children.

The numbers game

A combination of participant and non-participant observations over the year, alongside activities and conversations with groups of children (inside and outside the role-play areas), revealed a range of ways in which they tried to make sense of the social and pedagogical context. For example, children talked about how classroom rules and routines prevented them from playing. Jess explained: 'I don't like having to tidy up when you just want to finish playing, it's so annoying'. And Kate said she didn't like it when you have to 'put your hand up... [and teachers] only pick five ... [so] your friend has got to go out'. Joe also talked about '[having to] come out when it was too many'. When trying to negotiate particular situations, children themselves followed the rules that adults had set in place, for example the 'numbers rule':

Millie: Cheryl is the dad, I'm the mum ... stay there big brother ... (*to Alan*).
Kim to Millie: Can I play?
Millie: No there's three already.
Kim: I'm telling! (*Kim shouts over to researcher*) Julie, Millie won't let me in!
Researcher: Well Kim, Millie is choosing today, she has to decide.

Cheryl has now appeared from under the parachute and comes over to the researcher: 'Millie should say who's allowed in'. (Cheryl, at this point, seems to be testing the water with the researcher as 'the adult' to see what the reaction is. The researcher does not respond to Cheryl's comments.) Cheryl, echoing the researcher's earlier response, says to Kim: 'Kim, it's up to Millie. She can say who is allowed to come in'.

(Louis approaches the den and tries to go in.)

Millie:	No you can't come in, only two.
Louis:	No, four!
Millie:	Julie, it's only two isn't it?
Researcher:	I thought you said three just now, Millie.
Millie:	Yeah it was, but now only two.

Louis stands by the den with one foot in and one foot out. He won't 'disobey' Millie's ruling but he is not going quietly either. Louis is the youngest and the smallest boy in the class but this does not deter his aims when faced with bigger or older children. On this occasion he stands his ground and stays by the den.

In all three classrooms, the children used the 'number rule' in the same way, not simply, it would seem, to ensure that the class rule is applied fairly, but as a strategy to exclude other children. The number of children appeared to depend on the play 'leader's' feelings towards the person at the time and whether or not this would disrupt the game. For example, Millie misused the numbers rule to refuse Kim entry to the play. Sometimes as many as six or as few as two were allowed to enter. Children used this rule flexibly instead of directly saying 'no'.

What's in a theme?

Group discussions with the children engendered much debate about children's preferences for particular role-play themes.

Popstar:	Mums and dads actually, that's what I like.
Spike:	I like the travel shop, you can find nice places in the brochures.
Popstar:	We're learning things in school and then we play in there with them. Pet shop was my favourite ... I liked the vet not the shop, the animals were my favourite things ... the bears.
John and Spike:	We just played vets.
Spike:	Next time I think we are having a minibeast house.
Jessie to Popstar:	He likes the kitchen 'cos he can get naked in there!

Some themes were more popular than others and could be recalled several months later. For example, in one school the pirate ship was undoubtedly a big success, particularly for the boys. Six months later, many recalled vividly the games that they played.

Lena: You pretend playing something.
Nathan: 'cos when it's activity time it's fun to play in.
Harry: I liked the pirate ship best!
Lena: It's not good for us ... [Jack's cottage] it's a bit babyish. We like the pirate ship 'cos it's more grown up.
Michael: It's good for pirates ... we get treasure ... treasure box.
Harry: You could have a parrot on your shoulder.
Nathan: I really liked the talking parrot.
Michael: When we fight on the ship and swing on the ropes, we really like playing fighting don't we? Laura, we can swing on ropes and stuff!

The themes for role-play areas were selected on the whole by the teachers and, to a greater or lesser extent, in consultation with the children or with reference to what might interest them. In turn, the choice of theme was linked to the prescribed curriculum, and also to the acquisition of certain skills such as literacy and numeracy. By contrast, in the outdoor areas, children had freedom to choose the theme and nature of their role-play in negotiation with peers. Not surprisingly, the children rarely adhered to the role-play theme, gravitating to familiar domestic themes or using the designated role-play areas as private spaces for socialisation and talk. So what is the status of the role-play theme in early childhood settings? Some themes worked better than others, and were clearly more appealing to boys on the one hand, or girls on the other. All this raises important questions for the development of pedagogy. Teachers spend considerable time and energy on planning and resourcing elaborate role-play areas. Yet these are not always of interest to children and may even dissuade them from playing altogether, as was the case for Chloe and Kim. With this in mind we asked children to draw their favourite role-play theme and to talk about what in particular they liked about it.

'Drawing on gender'

Small groups of children were asked to draw their favourite role-play area. The children were then each asked to talk about their pictures while the researcher acted as scribe. We have presented the results in Table 5.1, illustrating the themes chosen according to gender.

As the table indicates, none of the boys chose to draw a 'house' or Mrs Grinling's Cottage as their favourite theme, although these were extremely

Table 5.1 Number of children by gender choosing favourite role-play theme

Role-play theme	Girls	Boys
Castle	3	2
House	10	0
Pirate ship	0	5
Pet shop	6	3
Travel agency	0	4
Jungle	2	3
Mrs Grinling's cottage	4	0
Spaceship	0	3

popular with the girls. Conversely, none of the girls chose the pirate ship, spaceship or travel agency, although these were popular with the boys. The children's choices may have been in part determined by the choices made by their friends. This method generated some useful data about the significance of particular themes, offering useful feedback for the teachers.

In the conversations with children about their pictures we were able to access more information about how children were constructing themselves in relation to gender. For example, in a conversation with Alfie he explained why he did not like the house role-play:

Alfie: We didn't like the house it was a girl's role-play.
Researcher: Why?
Alfie: Because it had flowers on it and the boys just didn't like it. *(Shaking his head.)*

There was not a significant difference between the numbers of boys or girls drawing either the castle or the jungle but there were marked differences in how the themes were represented in the pictures. Taking the castle as an example, the boys' pictures and accompanying narratives focused on fighting, battles and chopping people's heads off: strong aggressive, gory tales.

Sam {Boy aged
five, Castle, 3a}: I liked dressing up as a knight, I tried to kill a dragon and soldiers were killing it and I'm watching them battle. This is a soldier shooting his bow and arrow. This soldier's got one of those chains that you fly and it stabs the dragon. That's one of those sticks that they bang on the head like that *(demonstrates a 'club' action with his hand)*. Couldn't find gold so I did it yellow.
Researcher: Why did you want gold?
Sam: So as I could do the armour.

For the girls, however, the castle was represented in domestic/romantic narratives about 'mums and dads' or princesses living in the castle and a 'prince coming to the castle to marry all the princesses'. The girls also embellished their drawings with colour and decorative details. When Josie had finished her picture she decorated it around the edges. The researcher asked her what the pictures were around the edge and she replied, 'To make it look prettier'.

Shelly {Girl aged five, Castle, 3r}:   This boy's going to marry all the girls. And some plants in there. Girls are hiding away because they don't want to be married 'cos they don't like the boy. They've already been married, they're princesses. At the end they all decide to marry him.

The children's drawings and subsequent narratives added a further dimension to the data on children's perspectives. Through the children's drawings and the narratives that accompanied them we gained further insights into how these four- and five-year-olds were constructing and making sense of their experiences. As Browne (2004) argues, children are constrained (and enabled) by the range of experiences they have within the discourses available to them. Thus, adopting a dialogic approach with the children helped us to gain an understanding of what Browne suggests are the signs and symbols that children use to reflect and represent aspects of their gendered identities.

Figure 5.1 Castle, drawn by Sam (aged five)

Figure 5.2 Castle, drawn by Shelly (aged five)

Moving on

As the year progressed and friendships grew, the episodes of children's role-play lengthened, and as they 'grew' over the year so too did the length and complexity of their narratives. In this way, role-play performed a crucial function for children in their first year at school aligning with Perry's observations that 'pretend play with peers provides the opportunity for complex cognitive and social development' (2001: 8). Whilst some of the children had very strong imaginative skills and developed sophisticated stories in the course of their play, other children took time to get used to role-play and all that it entails. To illustrate, we include here an extended episode of role-play between two girls in the café. Roxanne is completely in control of the play, directing it as well as participating in it, moving in and out of the play frame, directing the play and organising the other children in the café in a confident, skilled way. Roxanne sustained her central role until she was called away to undertake a reading activity. Roxanne says 'You can pretend to take an order but you're not the baby'. She runs out of the café and says, 'Can I have a piece of paper please to go in the café?' She returns and says 'Right, what would you like, madam?' then pretends to write down the order. Mia also pretends to write it down and Roxanne interjects with, 'I'm the person that writes it down and you're in the kitchen and gives it out'. Turning her attention back to her customer, she asks, 'Right, what would you like to drink, madam?' Sally says 'I would like a doughnut' to which Mia replies, 'A doughnut'. Roxanne says 'No, Mia, don't tell her she doesn't know what there is ... I'll tell her, there's water. Orange juice and ice-cream. Do you want any cereal? She wants an ice-cream'. She gives the customer her food. Roxanne is now using the mobile phone and pretending to write down an order she says, 'Who's the mum, who's the mum? I'd like to have an order for some food but somebody's on the phone ... right, as soon as we can.' Roxanne says to Mary, 'Somebody's rung up and they want ten sausages, ten glasses of milk and ten ice-creams, they want it together, 'cos there's 10 of them all together'.

This extract provides a good illustration of the sociodramatic play as defined by Smilansky (1990) in Chapter 2, where groups of children negotiate a consensus of meaning with their peers regarding their roles and sustain their play over an extended period. We see here also the ebb and flow of role-play as it moves between children's alternative realities of what is real/not real.

As the project progressed, however, we noted that some children were moving away from certain types of role-play. For example, five weeks after the start of the term one of the teachers commented that the children had decided that they no longer wanted the role-play 'kitchen' anymore, so it was being moved to a different classroom so that the next role-play theme could be developed. At the same time some older children felt disgruntled when their younger counterparts were able to play and they had to undertake National Curriculum activities. On one occasion the teacher said only the younger children would be going outside to play. Toby, aged five, put up his hand and said: 'Can we [older children] go out?' The teacher replied, 'Not today, you will get a turn on another day. I want you to stay in and do an activity with me,' at which point there was a groan from several of the older children.

Lena, a Year 1 child in the combined reception and Year 1 class, clearly indicates that particular themes of play were not 'grown-up' enough for her: 'It's not good for us ... [Jack's cottage] it's a bit babyish. We like the pirate ship 'cos it's more grown up'.

The children themselves saw a line between the types of things they could do in the reception class as opposed to what school life would be like in Year 1. A teacher in one school mentioned that she had overheard the children talking that 'Year 1 is very hard and there wouldn't be any "play" when they went into Year 1'. It seemed that children themselves observed Year 1 children doing more difficult tasks or in some situations older children fuelled younger children's knowledge of what lay ahead of them in their next year at school. The researcher also had a conversation with James in which he told her he didn't want to go in to Year 1 and when asked why he said: 'They do really hard work in there'. When the researcher asked 'How do you know that, James?', he replied, 'Because my brother was in there and he told me about it'.

What these examples show us is how quickly the dichotomy between play and work becomes embedded in children's minds, a point that is well documented in the literature alongside evidence that play is often used as a holding task or as a reward for the completion of work (Fisher, 1996; Bennett *et al.*, 1997; Keating *et al.*, 2002; Pascal, 1990).

What did we learn from listening to the children?

From our reading of the children's comments, we identified a number of persistent themes, which we have described above. We conclude, however, with a few words on the actual experience of listening to children talk about their role-play. The first thing to note is how keen the children were to share their thoughts with us about play. This was evident in their enthusiasm for the task and obvious enjoyment in talking about play, arguably a rare opportunity in school. Their enthusiasm was perhaps in part due also to the social context of the group activities, in particular the opportunity to share with friends. We have emphasised the importance of appropriate child-centred methods in gathering meaningful data on their experiences.

One further factor that might usefully translate into considerations of pedagogical practice is how strongly the children felt about certain aspects of their role-play. As we have illustrated, they objected strongly to certain rules and routines that broke up their play, and cared deeply about who they played with. Finally, the children gave us important insights into their broader experiences of school, and into the social dynamics and peer culture of the classroom (Corsaro, 1997). For example, John stated that because there is role-play 'school is a better place'. Chloe's comments drew our attention to her sometimes difficult relationships with other girls: 'I don't like Rhia or Jane hitting me, pinching or pulling my hair'.

Pedagogical implications

Our conversations with the children, coupled with our observations of their interactions in role-play, reinforce the view that role-play performs a crucial social function for children in their first year at school and that 'pretend play with peers provides the opportunity for complex cognitive and social development' (Perry, 2001: 8). It is quite clear that some children have very strong imaginative skills and develop sophisticated stories in their play, while other children need time to develop and adjust to role-play in school and all that it entails. It is also a 'space' in which they can escape the demands of the formal curriculum and do what they told us they like to do: to pretend and to play with friends. What we have tried to do in this chapter is to outline the significant themes generated from the children's perspectives of role-play in their individual settings, which we hope will offer an added dimension to the wealth of literature that has looked at young children's experiences of role-play from the adults' perspective. Listening to children in this way could also function as an important tool for understanding how pedagogical practices impact upon the quality of children's play. We have touched on the issue of gender here since it arose in relation to children's preferred themes, which they articulated in the small group discussions. In the next chapter we develop the theme of gender more specifically in relation to pedagogy and teacher decisions about the organisation of space and place.

Chapter 6

Playing with space, place and gender

In this chapter we address two distinct but related themes that emerged from our analysis of the observational data on the interaction between children's role-play and the pedagogy of their classrooms. These are the gendered nature of children's role-play themes and their use of space and place. As in any ethnographic work, our aim must be to represent as fully as is possible the experiences of the research participants. We have tried to remain as open as possible to the children's interpretations of their experiences of role-play, and to give an honest and well-rounded interpretation of what we observed. The ways in which children chose to play were often at odds with adult expectations, including our own as researchers. This created tensions and dilemmas for the teachers, which resonate more widely in the field of early childhood education. We will refer to these throughout the chapter.

Gender in early childhood: tensions and dilemmas

There is a wealth of literature theorising young children's experiences of gender in educational settings (see Robinson and Jones Díaz, 2006; Browne, 2004; Skelton and Francis, 2003; MacNaughton, 2000; Yelland, 1998; Davies, 1989). Gendering occurs as an integral part of the routines of everyday life (Yelland and Grieshaber, 1998: 1) and by the time children have started school (in England and Wales at aged four or five) they are already constructing notions of gender from the familiar and the familial discourses within which they operate. From an early childhood standpoint, Browne offers the caveat that '[a] child is constrained by the range of experiences she has and her access to alternative discourses that would provide her with further options' (2004: 61). By suggesting this, she invokes the role of pedagogy and the responsibility of educators to widen the gender scripts of children in early childhood settings. Baxter argues that 'by the time children start school; both girls and boys have already begun to learn how to speak, read and write differently as a girl or a boy' (2001: 4). From our observational data we add 'play' to this list. Much of the play we observed reflected gender stereotypes, the girls displaying stereotypical notions of being a 'girl' by adopting mother/baby roles, dressing up as princesses, and acting out roles that involved emotional-caretaking behaviours. For the boys the play was predominantly about burglars, robbers, fire, police or superhero play. This is not surprising when we look at the forms of masculinity expressed in the 'superhero' discourse that is particularly appealing to boys (Marsh, 2000; Paley, 1984; Jordan, 1995). And we are not surprised by the degree to which children's play was threaded with these familiar and predictable themes. However, the prevalence of such themes in our observational data warrants closer consideration, particularly in relation to the pedagogical practices of the project classrooms.

Thorne (1993) rightly suggests that gender is not something one has or one is but rather it is something we continually create and recreate through social interaction and collective practices. Children are immersed in a culture of gendered symbols from the moment they take their first breath of life. The colours of their environment, their clothes and their toys as well as the language that is used to construct their worlds is gendered (Macguire, 1991). In primary schools the daily practices of children and adults sustain and give multiple meanings to the individual social categories 'girl' and 'boy' (Jordan, 1995). Children thus enter school as children (soon to become pupils) already equipped with notions of what it is to be either a 'boy' or a 'girl'. Dominant cultural discourses, whether in the school or elsewhere, offer particular ways of being a boy or a girl. Nowhere does this seem to be more apposite than in children's play.

Within early childhood theory and practice, discussions of children's development, relationships and behaviours oscillate between the natural and the social. The gendered dimensions of children's play have been portrayed through a wide range of analytical lenses including the biological, social constructionist, sex-role theories and poststructuralist accounts. Accounts from within education, including discussions with early childhood practitioners, often revert to the naturalising and the normalising behaviours based on biological gender differences (Robinson and Jones Díaz, 2006). For example, Patricia, a practitioner, comments: 'I know what you mean I have boys like that every year I've decided it's pointless trying to change nature' (MacNaughton, 2000: 11). This view was reflected in the language of our teachers too, in comments such as 'the boys need to be more active'. In the academic world (and particularly within sociological domains) 'essentialist versus constructionist' perspectives have been central to much of the discussion within the literature. Poststructuralist accounts offer a view of children learning how to 'do gender' by drawing on pre-existing discourses to express a notion of being either a boy or a girl (Davies, 1989). Other researchers claim that when entering school, young children may well initially exhibit non-stereotypical play but the normalising discourses of their peers soon offer them a clear picture of what is socially appropriate behaviour in relation to gender. Such are the contrasting views available to us. Gender plays are also power plays within school, thus the 'micro politics' of power through play are significant (Blaise, 2005; Campbell *et al.,* 2004; Scales, 1996; Thorne, 1993; Francis, 1998, cited in Arnot, 2002).

Within early childhood practice in the UK and elsewhere, an additional gender dimension is also worth considering here. The vast majority of adults in settings for young children are female, and this is likely to shape pedagogical practices in significant ways. Research suggests that the predominant female perception has been that boys' play is noisy, physical and disruptive (Holland, 1999). This view ultimately positions female teachers at an impasse as to how best to respond to and deal with this kind of play. One of the ways in which female staff may address boys' play is to feminise the environment by eliminating these 'masculine' behaviours altogether. Swain (2004), for example, alerts us to the many difficulties teachers face by 'banning' activities associated with particular forms of masculinity. In one school, Swain noted that the head teacher had banned football as a playground activity because she had deemed it to be expressing the 'wrong' form of masculinity. Banning football did not result in the disappearance of macho forms of activities; rather the boys invented a range of alternative activities that simply reinforced macho forms of masculinity based on corporeal skills such as speed and strength. Clearly, children also have agency and are not always inclined to accept passively what is meted out to them. In the context of their role-play, our children employed similarly subversive techniques to those identified by Swain.

For example, a group of boys is dressed as pirates, preparing to embark on a mock battle. In the absence of any guns, Seth picks up a stick and starts using it as a gun, pointing and shooting. He is dressed in stripy pirate t-shirt, headscarf, eye-patch and leather belt, which has his 'gun' [stick] and telescope in it. James offers Seth a necklace: 'Here's a necklace for you', but Seth says in a very gruff voice, 'Get off me'. All three boys now have sticks that they are using as guns. Seth says, 'Who wants to be in my team?' They all shout 'Me!'. Seth chooses two boys to be in his gang. All the pirates are now 'shooting' at each other with their 'guns'. The pirates lie dead on the ship's deck. Joe says to Sean: 'You're dead already'. Sean retorts, 'No, I'm not dead', but Joe, pointing to the floor says, 'You are, look at the blood'.

The noise level continues to rise as the boys become completely immersed in their game. The gun play with sticks has completely taken over the play theme and the play area. In another part of the room the teacher stands up. Joe sees her and says, 'Uh, oh'. He tries to run away as he knows that the teacher is cross. The teacher intervenes, stopping the gun play by telling the boys that they are 'not to use the sticks as guns, the sticks are there to build the ship'. The teachers' intervention effectively stops the play. Once the thread of the play is lost, it is difficult for the boys to continue so the play dis-integrates completely and the boys disperse.

On this occasion it could be argued that the teacher had adopted a policy of zero tolerance in her classroom, which she applied to this example of role-play between the boys. At the same time the play was noisy and boisterous and was beginning to spill over into other activities, thus disturbing other children who were working. So on two counts, the play was unacceptable within the pedagogical framework of the classroom. Zero tolerance approaches towards aggressive elements of play and in particular 'gun play' have been adopted widely in schools and early childhood settings, often for good ethical and educational reasons. In her book on gun play, Holland (1999) reflects on the 'zero tolerance' approach she adopted towards aggressive forms of play. Clearly the rule applied to both boys and girls. Yet, inevitably, in practice the rule was applied far more frequently to the play of boys than that of the girls. It is interesting to note the absence of any such rule that explicitly, or implicitly for that matter, would apply in the same way to the play of girls. Holland concluded that the outlawing of aggressive forms of play simply led to an escalation of conflict between the adults and the boys. On the other hand, relaxing this approach and allowing boys to incorporate elements of playful aggression into their narratives encouraged them to engage in more extended bouts of 'free-flow dramatic play'. Already we can detect a tension developing between the gendered behaviours of children and discourses of developmentalism. We may opt to administer policies in the name of the theories and values we hold, but clearly the reality of classroom life is much more complex and more nuanced.

The examples considered so far suggest that the ways in which boys and girls play is a thorny issue which needs vigilance and reflection on the part of teachers and researchers alike. Rather than banning particular forms of play, a more fruitful approach may be to open up dialogue with young children about what they play and how they play. As previous studies have identified, banning particular activities not only makes them more appealing but often does little more than subvert the outlawed activity or behaviour (Swain, 2004; Holland, 1999). Of course, it was not only the boys who engaged in role-play that presented adults with pedagogical tensions and dilemmas. Remembering the example of Kim and Chloe in Chapter 5, and their out-right resistance to the requests of adults, we can see that subversion is not gender-specific.

A further dilemma was presented in relation to the girls' play, which was as starkly 'feminine' as the boys' was 'masculine'. The point has been made already that girls almost always played in some way or another with domestic themes and roles and most commonly at being mothers. With our adult fem-inist hats on, we reflected on how their role-play scripts might be widened to incorporate more diverse and more challenging roles. But in the face of numerous rich examples of play about mothers, we grappled equally with the question 'So what's wrong with gender stereotypical play when you are four years old?' To highlight the dilemma facing all early childhood educators we give an extended example of the play world of one child, whom we call Annie. In her play she explored conventional notions of motherhood: caring for babies, siblings, juggling household chores with family, to name but a few. Her persistence and determination to play the role of mother to her dolls, sometimes to the exclusion of all other activities, was such that it generated some important discussions around how far we should intervene in the choices and play preferences of young children.

Annie's story

Annie unwittingly became an icon for the project, partly because she challenged our adult conceptions of gender identity and practices in early childhood, but also because her persistence in playing the role of 'mother' raised important pedagogical issues for the teachers. In fact Annie played at being mother to her dolls for a period of nine months, beginning on her first day at school and ending sometime in May of the following year.

Annie's story is useful in terms of looking at the inherent pedagogical difficulties of resolving the tension that inevitably exists between the 'individual' personality and needs and the 'structural' elements of education. Annie was just four years old when we met her, arriving in a reception class at the start of the school year. From the start she played with dolls that she said were her 'babies'. At that time Annie preferred to play on her own (or at least in a position where she was in control of the play story). When playing outside, Annie always engaged in the same routine. First, she collected her 'babies' and then would walk around with them in a wicker basket or pram. She would ask for blankets to put on the ground for her 'babies' to sit on. On one occasion while waiting patiently for the Year 1 children to start a Punch and Judy show, Annie could be seen sitting on a wooden block with a headscarf on and her arms around a doll on each side of her, talking to them at length about the show they were about to see. One of the ways in which we listened to children's views about role-play was to ask them to take pictures of the things that mattered to them in school. We include Annie's photograph as Figure 6.1.

> As the weeks progressed, Annie continued to carry her dolls everywhere, but she also began to transform other scenarios into the 'mummies and babies' discourse. For example, when playing with dinosaurs at the small world drama table, Annie said 'go sleep babies'. Dad (the biggest dinosaur of them all) is carrying four or five little dinosaurs (babies) on his back with 'mummy' at his side. Annie showed me the middle-sized

dinosaur and told me, 'They are brother and sister'. On one occasion she said: 'They [the babies] go off on a lovely sunny day, but not the mummy or daddy' and 'the baby dinosaurs going off to the river to play with their [older] brother and sister'. Narrative is an important correlate of pretence and helps children to internalise their ideas about the world. In this kind of play, children become absorbed in the imaginary world, forget the self and the passing of time, all of which make the world out-side 'vanish'. On another occasion Eve and Annie have headscarves on and Annie is carrying her baby around with her. Annie lays out a blan-ket and a pillow on the grass for her baby to lie down on. Having decided to watch the Punch and Judy show, Annie moves the blanket and the pillow next to her on the seating in the audience, she puts the baby to bed and tucks her up. When Leanne announces the show is about to start, Annie, who now has another baby, picks up both babies and sits them one each side of her with her arms around them waiting for the show to start. Annie is wandering around with her 'babies' and asks the researcher to find a blanket for her so that she can sit her babies on it. Annie always starts off her play with her babies, they usually end up in a basket, from which she removes them and puts them on a blan-ket on the ground or the grass bank.

(Field notes)

Figure 6.1 Annie's doll, taken by Annie

Annie continued her doll narrative throughout the school year and was captured in photographs and on video footage with her 'babies' and their blankets. Then one day in May, we noticed that she had spent the whole of the outdoor play session without her doll and her blankets. We were not sure at this stage if it was just a 'one-off', but the following week the teacher also commented that Annie was no longer playing with her dolls.

Annie's story raises the following questions:

- Should the teacher have intervened in Annie's doll narrative and tried to attract her into different forms of role-play?
- Is it educationally justifiable to move young children on into roles they do not choose for themselves?
- From a pedagogical standpoint, how could the teacher have widened Annie's gender script whilst allowing for her individual developmental and social needs to be met?

Annie's teacher was alive to issues of gender equity within her classroom. She made a deliberate decision neither to intervene in Annie's free play nor to forbid her from bringing her dolls to other activities. The dolls, she argued, were transitional objects (Winnicott, 1971; Bruce, 1989) and Annie's play was meaningful and relevant for her at that particular time. We have seen already how Holland (1999) noted the difficulties inherent in banning particular forms of play for boys, such as gun play. We want to offer a similar platform from which to reflect upon and debate the persistent themes in the role-play of girls. We use Annie as a case study, to exemplify the theme of 'mothering' since it was the predominant type of play observed in all three classrooms.

The dilemma facing early childhood educators of whether or not to intervene is discussed widely in the literature but the debate tends to be adult- rather than child-focused. Given that the central aim of the project was to understand role-play from the children's perspectives, how might we deconstruct children's expression of gender through a child-focused lens? Arnot *et al.* (1999, cited in Arnot, 2002: 258) offer a useful reminder that 'schools will need to listen to male and female pupils to learn how far and in what ways boys and girls have different ways of knowing and of learning a diversity of gender identities'.

Mothers in space

Annie's play around the themes of motherhood highlights a common preoccupation in the play of girls. However, these domestic themes were expressed in a range of different ways in different role-play contexts. To illustrate how gendered roles unfold alongside and within other less gender-specific roles, we give an example of play in the spaceship. Initially, the children adopt the roles of astronauts, 'spaceman' and 'spacegirl'. However, the narrative takes an unexpected turn when both boys and girls gravitate towards more overtly stereotypical play.

Spaceman:	Quick we need to change direction, I directioned it!
Spacegirl (blowing through plastic tube):	Ring ring *(speaking in to it giving other end of pipe to spaceman)*. We're going to crash.
Spaceman:	We're going the other way now, mum; I need to switch them all off now to change direction. *(Proceeds around the spaceship pressing all the control pads to reschedule the spaceship.)* No, we're going to crash, I can't do it, we're still going to crash in the rock. *(Spaceman speaks into the telephone.)* Ring, ring we're going to crash. Press the green one, Spacegirl.
Flower:	Are we crashing into a big rock?
Spaceman:	No, we're not, we're crashing into another rocket!
Flower and Spacegirl:	We're the spacegirls *(giggling)*.
Spaceman:	Be quiet I'm trying to do my homework.
Flower:	Some of my friends are coming to tea.
Spaceman:	No, I'm the boss you've got to tell me first!
Spacegirl:	I'm the cousin.
Flower:	I know you are, darling. *(The girls have taken the plastic discs off the wall which were 'control pads' for the spaceship and are using them as plates to lay up for Spacegirl's birthday tea!)*
Spacegirl:	It's my birthday today.
Flower:	Yes it is, my darling.
Spaceman:	I'm not watching you open your presents then 'cos it's not fair.
Flower:	Be nice to your sister then.

When 'Spaceman' cannot get his own way in directing the play he assumes a self-imposed authority role; in short, he slips into hegemonic masculinity mode (Connell, 1987): 'I'm the boss!' This attempt however does nothing to avert the girls' emphasis on domesticity and the theme of the 'birthday party'. Even where the themes suggest to children wider and more varied scripts, both boys and girls draw on their knowledge and experience of what it means to be male or female. Although the play quickly reverts to more familiar gendered themes, it clearly involves much more than the simple reproduction of roles. Children play what they know, but to do so in the context of shared pretence, drawing on and transforming experience, is a complex and remarkable feat. Domestic play is more important to young children than we sometimes recognise in our efforts to make role-play more interesting and more relevant to the curriculum. Within apparently mundane domestic scenarios, the complexities of relationships, daily routines and events are played out, varied and embellished, social dynamics are tested and rehearsed, and social bonds are established and terminated. These are all vitally important experiences for young children. Domestic themes are likely to be popular and relevant to children at this age because they are familiar and safe. In role-play, children are free to experiment and explore alternative domestic scenarios. Only rarely do they act out scenes that are identical to those they have experienced at home, rather they are representations of children's lives. This is Vygotsky's point (1978). Children interpret and rework familiar scripts to fit their immediate play needs. In this way, whatever the theme or role adopted in the play it is always a creative, imaginative and interpretive process.

In the following examples, we see children drawing on a myriad of experiences and discourses in the context of their role-play:

(Georgina is at the computer typing on the keyboard and writing in the log book.)
Georgina: I need Shaun to get off the phone!
Shaun: I'm not Shaun, I'm Spiderman.
Max: I'm a Jedi knight. They are better than aliens because they have green, blue and wed [red] lightsavers [lightsabres] and they are the best.

What we see here with Georgina is interaction and negotiation: 'I need Shaun to get off the phone', whilst Shaun and Max slip clearly into 'role': 'I'm not Shaun, I'm Spiderman' and 'I'm a Jedi knight', good examples of children being able to slip between fantasy and reality, which for Shaun and Max encompasses the populist and popular superhero play theme.

Children interpreted role-play themes in different ways. The following example of mixed-gender play shows the different ways in which the boys and girls made sense of a story about Mrs Grinling's cottage and the roles they adopted amongst themselves. For readers who are not familiar with the story, Mrs Grinling is trying to get lunch to her husband, the lighthouse keeper.

> Harriet picks up Hamish the 'cat' and she holds him on her hip in the way that an adult female often holds a baby. She looks at him and says 'he's wet', meaning that his bottom is wet. She then holds him over the fence of the play house and says 'he needs to do a pee now' and laughs. When the play session has finished, Harriet calls the researcher to show her how she has tidied up the cottage, with all the baskets placed neatly on the floor. Harriet has firmly adopted the role of 'mother', providing the food and looking after Hamish. The boys did not seem as engaged with the 'cottage' theme but set about planning to prevent the seagulls from stealing the lighthouse keeper's lunch. To do this they made an 'electric fence' by tying some string across the front of the cottage. The seagulls would fly into the

electric fence, which would kill the gulls. As well as constructing an electric fence, the boys strategically placed Sellotape near the fence as a second line of defence. The girls were busily preparing the food and looking after Hamish the cat, the boys adopted the role of problem solvers and 'protectors' to prevent the gulls from stealing the food so the girls could get the food to its destination.

(Field notes)

In these examples, we see the many ways in which the children are positioned by multiple discourses of gender, practised within particular contexts and communities (Paechter, 2003; Skelton, 2001). As Steedman (1987) concludes in *The Tidy House*, the working-class girls offer small insights into how they are drawing on their own experiences and circumstances to confront what might lie ahead of them; in short, these children are undertaking roles that they experience in their home lives and their wider communities. Children's expression of gender was not confined to the roles they adopted in their play. Often children revealed their understanding of gender in their interactions with one another of not just their personal experience but also what they may have observed. In the following examples, we see how dominant gendered behaviours and attitudes shape how children play together. In the first example, the researcher is part of the play with Daniel and Hannah. Daniel reveals his understanding of what is and is not possible for men and women in the workplace. He plays at being the boss man, exerting his authority and power in the game, shown in Figure 6.2, through his physical posture.

Figure 6.2 Daniel in the travel shop (feet on desk)

Daniel says, 'We're from the council but she's not' (pointing to Hannah) 'she's the lady'. I ask Daniel if she is the lady from the council to which he replied indignantly: 'No, she can't be from the council, she's a lady. We're from the council, me and him' (pointing to Piers).

(Field notes)

Billy to Ria and Laura: Who's the mother?
(The girls ignore him.)
Billy: Who's the mother?
Researcher: You be the mother, Billy.
Billy (shakes his head
and laughs):   No!

Children also revealed their understanding of gender in conversation with the researchers. For example:

Rebecca starts to tell me about all the things that she has had for Christmas and asks me to write them down in my notebook. Kelly then appears and asks me to do the same for her. Eloise insists that I cannot write Kelly's things down on the same page. After I had written the lists I gave the girls their pieces of paper. Kelly then says, 'Shall I write down all the things my brother had, he's one?' I ask, 'Did he have a talking doll?' [the present that Kelly had]. Kelly laughs and says, 'No, he's a boy, he doesn't have a doll'. When I ask, 'Why is that, Kelly?' she replies 'Only an Action Man not a doll'.

(Field notes)

In the following two examples the boys are subjected to the normalising forces of peer culture when they try to step outside the acceptable boundaries of their gender role:

Dan has arrived in the spaceship and says: 'I'm going to put a girl's dress on'. [This is the first time I have ever seen a boy do this in any school.] Alice exclaims, 'That's a girl's dress!' Dan throws the dress in the box and says: 'I'm not putting it on', the inference being he was joking.

Billy has just spotted Spike in his pink fairy dress and pink hat and he laughs loudly and then shouts across the playground: 'Look at this girl, Ms Colby, look at this girl!' Spike immediately takes his hat off and throws it on the floor and then runs inside. [Spike was perfectly okay wandering around in his pink outfit until 'peer pressure' via Billy's gendered commenting put Spike in the limelight ... very powerful example of the hegemonic discourse and the heteronormative process of boys' roles/behaviours.]

(Field notes)

These are strong examples of how children are subject to scrutiny from their peers early on in their school lives. They also serve as an illustration of Thorne's (1993) point that boys are doubly disadvantaged when they step out of their gender position, as they are also seen to be transgressing their sexuality, a factor that appears to be more difficult for boys than for girls.

Space and place

We move on to consider some of the ways in which the children utilised space and place in their play and the relationship of this to classroom pedagogy. Since the introduction of the *Curriculum Guidance for the Foundation Stage* (QCA, 2000) in England and Wales, there has been a renewed drive to improve the quality of play provision in early childhood settings. This is evidenced most obviously in the development of outdoor spaces for play, and the expanding research and policy literature on the subject. There has been far less consideration of how indoor spaces might be reconceived in order to meet the curriculum objectives of the Foundation Stage and the identified needs of children aged three to five. This is especially the case for the reception classes of primary schools, which cater for the majority of four-year-olds in England. Clearly, the organisation and use of space in classrooms is culturally, socially and economically determined, reflecting also the pedagogical priorities of the educational community in general, and individual practitioners in particular.

It has long been acknowledged that space, or lack of it, may have negative outcomes for children's behaviour and well-being. Siraj-Blatchford and Sylva go further to identify a negative correlation between restrictions on indoor space and children appearing 'anti-social, worried and upset' (2004: 719). Buildings, outside play areas and furnishings have an effect on the well-being of the child. Children of different ages have different spatial requirements. For example, children of five and six may need more individual space and privacy than toddlers (van Liempd, 2005: 17). In the project classrooms, the role-play areas were often used by the children as private spaces. The children's physical size also influenced how they used space. A severe lack of space in two of the three project classrooms impacted significantly on what and how the children could play. Lack of space was further complicated in one of these classrooms where reception children were grouped with Year 1 children. This meant that some children were engaged for much of the time in National Curriculum activities in close proximity to the role-play area. The teacher described how this impacted on the children's role-play:

> [the] smallness of the environment, and they're involved in some noisy play, and they're working beside a group of children who are trying to do some writing or whatever, it's got to be restricted because, you know, they're going to be disturbing the children who are doing the writing activity and that's just the nature of the mixed year group.

We noted that the use of classroom space differed significantly for boys, on the one hand, and girls, on the other. Role-play areas occupied a small corner in each of the classrooms and could accommodate about four children. Thus, the areas set aside for role-play were relatively small when compared to those used for more formal activities. As Frost *et al.* (1998) remind us, the physical arrangement of a room conveys a symbolic message to children about what might happen in a particular place. Furthermore, in early childhood settings the way in which space for role-play areas is demarcated, allocated and valued in relation to the rest of classroom space clearly sends out a message to children about which activities have more or less value (Fisher, 2001). More 'formal' educational activities, such as those relating to literacy and numeracy, often appeared to be more important since children were frequently asked to moderate their role-play behaviour and reduce noise levels as these were having a detrimental effect on other children's concentration in the classroom.

Colonising and controlling space

There were some marked distinctions along gendered lines in children's differential use of space. Many of the boys we observed in the project persistently appeared to use as much space in the classroom as they were able to in the course of their play. Boys tended to move beyond the physical boundaries of the role-play far more frequently and more extensively than the girls, whose play tended to stay within the confines of the designated role-play area in the classroom. Newson and Newson's (1968) study of four-year-olds in urban environments concluded that attitudes to the use of space are set long before children enter school. Girls, in particular, are encouraged from a young age by their parents to stay within the confines of the home. Conversely, boys are expected to be more adventurous and are given more spatial freedom, and, they argue, more psychological freedom (cited in Bhatti, 1999).

Space for role-play in the classroom was carved up by the children along gendered lines. We found that the boys in the project controlled far more of the space than the girls (see also Thorne, 1993 cited in Jordan, 1995). Colonising space meant invading the girls' space for some boys. There were many instances of boys deliberately disrupting the play of girls, barging in and taking over play spaces. According to MacNaughton (1992) this can be seen as seen as boys using their physical power to control space. To give an example, in the following episode a group of girls had been playing for twenty minutes when a group of boys physically invaded the space in an attempt to take over the role-play area. Paige tried to stop the boys entering and Sharon tried to add further resistance, but the boys took no notice:

Paige: Boys aren't allowed in here!
Lucy: He's a robber; he steals all your money.

Sharon: Hey, you can't come in here, it's our secret hideout.
Jake: Yes we can!
Michael: Don't let the baddies see this.

Interestingly, the use of physical power to control play spaces is coupled with an apparent desire on the part of the boys to join the girls' play. They do this by weaving a new theme into the girls' narrative. The girls attempt to protect their interactive space (Cosaro, 1997), but to no avail.

In a second example, a group of girls had been playing happily in a den, developing their story through their play. A group of boys entered. Suddenly, one of the boys started 'crashing' about inside the den. The den collapsed and the play narrative was lost. On this occasion the girls didn't react at all to the boys' disruptive entrance. Although they were clearly frustrated with Jake, they did not challenge him. When the researcher asked the girls what happened to the den, Annie replied: 'Jake came in and he broke it all'.

Containing play

Related to lack of classroom space is the pedagogical strategy that we call 'containing play'. By this we mean the way in which children's play is constrained, not only by space, but by organisational, physical and social factors in the classroom. Containing play is both an issue for teachers and an inhibiting factor for the role-play of boys in particular. For example, Cathy (teacher) comments 'the bigger space outside means they [boys] won't be as constrained as they inevitably are inside the classroom'. The containment of play seemed to affect the boys more overtly than the girls as it was often the boys who had to change the nature of their play to meet the demands of the adults and the classroom environment. Our observations raised some important questions about the nature of play in school. At times children's play, and especially boys' play, exceeds the boundaries of what is deemed acceptable behaviour in the classroom. The teachers recognised that role-play is by its nature often noisy and physical. Yet at the same time such play presented the teachers with a problem regarding its potentially disruptive influence on classroom life:

> They [boys] need to be more active. We have this shop front which is a
> small thing you get inside of and the boys are a nightmare they end up
> destroying it because it is too confining. The 'space' has to be big enough
> to create their own 'stamp' and for the boys to be less destructive. Boys'
> play does tend to be more boisterous, when it is a home or a shop there is
> usually a burglar that the boys have to run around and catch or it is
> superhero type of play.

By contrast, we found that in all three project classrooms the girls tended to contain their own play, rarely coming into situations of conflict with the adults around them. This is not unproblematic as it raises questions about why the girls appear to be so compliant. Much of the role-play we observed between girls in the classroom involved sitting in pairs or small groups within the specified role-play area, chatting about shared interests (popular culture, for example, Rapunzel, Barbie, friendship and families), drawing and painting. It was clear that children's 'creative' use of classroom space and noisy play could not easily be sanctioned in project classrooms and, as we saw in Chapter 4, compelled adults to intervene. We would also go so far as to suggest that this 'containment' affects boys more than girls and starts to set the pattern of their getting into conflict situations with their teachers and teaching assistants (usually women) at a very early age (see Marsh, 1999).

Moving boundaries

In Chapter 5 we described how the children challenged adults' requests and classroom rules. Children were also active in their responses to the use of space for role-play and made significant and unsanctioned changes to their environment in order to pursue their role-play interests. Children repositioned the boundaries of their role-play, either literally or by simply extending their play beyond the role-play area to places that were out of bounds. In one example, in an episode of travel agency play, the mixed-gender group of children decided to establish a train station in the opposite corner of the classroom. However, travel between the two areas meant running between tables and chairs where other groups of children were working. Clearly, this was disruptive and difficult to accommodate, but the children pursued the game until an adult finally intervened. In the project group meetings with the teachers, we reflected on the structural features of pedagogy that indirectly regulate children's behaviour in this and other ways. We posed the question, 'How might we be able to understand the issue of space from the children's perspective?' The teachers were aware that lack of indoor space was a major inhibiting factor in developing their role-play in the directions they wanted. But making substantial changes to the organisation of internal space was just not an option, as we saw in Chapter 4. Developing the outdoor area was seen as a means of reducing the need to contain play, as one teacher explained:

> We now have our outside area as well, so that's moved some of the space issue and the noise kind of thing that might occur ... so that it isn't such a constraint that it may have been a year ago.

In this school, developing the outdoor area had been seen as a means of reducing the need to contain play:

We now have our outside area as well so that's loved some of the space issue and the noise kind of thing that might occur ... so that it isn't such a constraint that it may have been a year ago.

A second question to emerge for all participants was how we might better accommodate the needs of both boys and girls in relation to use of classroom space. For boys the issue seemed to be a lack of space in which to express their play needs and interests. But more than that, lack of space and the containment that this engenders appeared to create a tension between boys and their educators and perhaps exacerbated further their apparent need to be active. For girls the issues are rather different. There is undoubtedly great concern about meeting the needs of boys' physical and educational learning approaches, yet there has been little reflection on girls' continued 'compliance' towards the routines of classroom life. Holland (2003) suggests that such compliance may well set the scene for the taking up of passive female roles in the future lives of the girls. If we are to develop a pedagogy of play in early childhood, how would we ensure that this was a gender-equitable process within classroom settings that encourage girls and boys to step beyond the heteronormative frameworks they are already socialised within? We hold that there is a need to encourage girls to take on more active and proactive roles in their play, for as we have seen, there were times when they found the role-play of boys was both intimidating and destructive. At the same time, some reflection on the uses (and abuses) of space might lead to creating play areas that allow both boys and girls to express their play interests more fully.

Outdoor solutions

Play has a strong physical dimension for young children, whether it takes the form of running, chasing and rolling or simply playing in close physical proximity to other children. This may also include physical contact with each other. Outdoor play enables children to stretch their physical capabilities, and to expand their imaginations into the realms of physical actions. For example, in one episode of outdoor play a child may need to run to escape from the wolf – this would be difficult if not impossible to do in the classroom, yet for the integrity of the story, running away is important. Physical play enables children to explore their 'comfort zones' – how close they want to be to individual children – to explore the boundaries of friendships. Such physical actions may be part of the play, for example in a pretend 'accident' or 'fire', or they may simply be for the pleasure of being close to someone in a den, hiding together, wrestling or pretend fighting. Many species of young animals frequently engage in this type of important play activity as a way of rehearsing actions that will be useful in later life. We often hear early childhood educators say that boys need to be physical in their learning. This is true also for girls, of

Figure 6.3 Exploring the boundaries

course; they may not always choose the physical option, but in our experience of this project, they are more likely to engage in building, running and climbing if they are outside.

There is a dearth of literature on the effects of the outdoor play environment on nurturing children's play culture and play behaviour (Frost *et al.,* 1998). The literature that is available demonstrates clearly the benefits of the outdoor environment (for example, Bilton, 1997; Perry, 2001; Stephenson, 2002) and this is now more evident in practice. The general consensus is that children should be able to access a free-flow from the 'indoor to the outdoor' environment (Stephenson, 1998; Isenberg and Quisenberry, 2002). However, a lack of adequate outdoor play remains a challenge for many primary school reception classes in England and Wales (Staggs, 2004).

Stephenson's (1998) work further identifies that boys in particular choose to be outdoors, whilst others raise the difficulty surrounding children's differential use of outdoor play space in relation to gender (Garrick, 2004). However, Shin (1994) and Shin and Frost (1995) (both cited in Frost *et al.,* 1998), conclude that irrespective of gender, children spent more time engaging in dramatic play in outdoor settings, and their play themes were more diverse outdoors than indoors. This was our experience in the project.

From a child's perspective it is quite clear that being outdoors (even if wet) is important (Petrie *et al.,* 2000). For example, Mooney and Blackburn (2003) concluded in their consultation with children: 'Children like playing outside ... All children disliked restrictions being placed on outdoor play' (21). In the project we also had first-hand evidence of children wanting to engage with the outdoor environment. We saw Toby in Chapter 5 complaining that only the younger children in the class were allowed to play outside on that particular day. Jake, also one of the older boys who was involved in a literacy task, pleaded with his teacher, 'can we go outside?'

In the project schools, outdoor spaces undoubtedly gave children some time away from the adult gaze and provided children with greater opportunities for independence than in indoor adult-defined and regulated spaces (Baldock, 2001, cited in Garrick 2004). The outdoor environment also encouraged children to build 'dens'. Any type of structure could be turned into 'den' play. This seemed to appeal to children, first because they were able to create their own spaces, and second, because it enabled them to escape the adult 'gaze'. Dens also enabled a larger number of children to play together in small spaces. Restrictions that applied indoors, such as the 'only four' ruling, did not apply outdoors.

In one example, there was a small wooden house in the outdoor area. Several children were sitting inside it and told the researcher that they were going to a friend's wedding party (Figure 6.4). One child was dressed as a bride with a veil over her head. Robert found a cloth and pulled it over the roof of the house and said to the others inside, 'You're trapped'. The researcher asked: 'What's the cloth for?' to which Robert replied, 'We don't want anyone to see us'.

Figure 6.4 'Wedding party'

Whilst outdoor environments may not solve the problem completely because of weather conditions, outdoor play served to 'free up' both teachers and children from the confinement of their indoor environment. For children who were new to school, 'widening' the available spaces for children's role-play allowed them to stay on the margins of the play until they had worked out the routines of the outdoor environment and how to access the play. This was more difficult indoors where numbers were limited and children were also engaged in adult-intensive tasks. White *et al.* (1995) found that young children often seek out places of seclusion and privacy, particularly on the margins of outdoor spaces, away from the invasion of others. Our study also highlighted the benefits of having access to an outdoor environment in which the children had the space to go off and find an area where they could play by themselves or integrate socially to whatever degree they wanted to. Outside there was also a wide range of open-ended resources that appealed to different children's individual tastes. In one school, the researcher noted fourteen different activities available for children to choose that required minimal intervention from adults.

Outdoor areas also help with other pedagogical factors; for example, Joe, a large-framed boy with additional learning needs often ended up in conflict situations in indoor role-play settings, but outdoors he integrated well and played for extended periods of time without interruption or the need for adult intervention. The freedom of the extended space outside offered children the flexibility and the freedom to develop their own play themes, rather than being adult-directed, which appeared to add to the creativity of their narratives.

It is suggested here that play, and particularly role-play, can act as a powerful vehicle for exploration of gender practices in early childhood settings and can be used to offer alternative discourses to the gender-stereotypical roles that children so often keenly re-enact. Through intervention, teachers can encourage boys to experiment with different versions of masculinity (see Jordan, 1995), and equally we should be offering girls alternative femininity scripts.

As other studies have demonstrated (Blaise, 2005; Campbell *et al.*, 2004; MacNaughton, 2000; Davies, 1989; Thorne, 1993), there is a need for schools to identify the dominant modes of masculinity and femininity operating within their environment and to develop appropriate strategies accordingly. As we have argued, there are tensions between disrupting children's interests in the name of equity practices and recognising the nature of role-play in children's early development. Pedagogical strategies may well need to allow children to adopt Holland's (1999) notion of 'writing their own play scripts'. Annie's story is a case in point, widening her play script in her own time. As children make the transition from home to pre-school or school, through their experiences of the social world and the wider discourses within which they operate, they may well adopt stereotypically gendered play. Over time, however, given certain environmental and pedagogical factors, children are likely to move beyond their traditional roles. In addition, by developing and opening up the outdoor environment, teachers and children can be liberated from the confinement of their indoor environment. In turn, this appeared to impact favourably on boys' use of space in their role-play.

Evidence from our study indicates that outdoor play areas enable children to create play spaces for themselves and to exercise greater choice over materials, location and playmates. This encourages girls to take on more active roles and engage in more construction activities as part of their role-play (such as building towers, the perimeters of a house or hospital), and we noted that boys engaged more frequently in writing and more overtly social activity such as planning play narratives together (Figures 6.5, 6.6 and 6.7). As a result of this, we observed far fewer disruptive behaviours in the outdoors, and fewer instances of conflict with adults. Ultimately this must be the 'space and place' we aim for in early childhood settings.

As other studies demonstrate, outdoor play is qualitatively different from indoor play. Fewer restrictions and control over behaviour and resources results in outdoor play being more flexible and open-ended (Stephenson, 2002). The data from this study fully support this and it seems to be a real opportunity for widening not just children's physical environments but, in terms of gender, possibly their social vistas too.

Figure 6.5 Outdoor writing

Figure 6.6 Girls building a tower

Conclusion

In connection with the indoors, we have identified some of the ways in which adults 'contain' and censor children's role-play. We also outlined some of the key distinctions between the gendered dimensions of the play behaviours, play themes and types of interactions with others that children displayed in both their indoor and outdoor role-play. We also raised issues for further debate about how we can accommodate play in early childhood settings for all children, which, for boys in particular, is often executed on a large scale, and is highly physical and noisy. Such play is contained by adults and, as we shall see, can lead to conflict between boys and their female educators. We are not in any way operating within a 'poor boys discourse' (see Epstein *et al.*, 2002), which has tended to dominate government agendas over the past decade. Nor

Figure 6.7 Boys planning play

are we looking to essentialise the discussion. We are equally concerned about the 'compliance' of girls in early childhood. We are aware that play is a critical site of gender construction and a significant site of heteronormative processes (Robinson and Jones Díaz, 2006). We have focused in this chapter on some of the dominant play behaviours and roles observed in the project classrooms. However, we are not suggesting that all our boys were the 'fighting boys' described by Jordan (1995). Many boys also enjoyed quiet activities and did not exceed the boundaries of acceptable classroom behaviour. Nor were all the girls 'Barbie' girls or mother figures. One final caveat on this matter: our aim here is not to generalise, but to describe the settings in which the research was conducted, and in so doing to encourage debate amongst practitioners and academics about the reality of accommodating children's interests with equity practice in early childhood educational settings.

The practitioners engaged with this study were alive and receptive to the hegemonic processes at play within their environments, but they were also concerned with children's individual gender scripts. We must also not forget that children themselves have agency in what and how they play and even when 'gender neutral' role-play areas are offered, children often subvert their play in order to develop their own themes and narratives. We concur with Campbell *et al.* (2004: 84) 'that there is not one single right or true theory that can guide equity praxis in early childhood classrooms ... [c]lassroom life is complex and multifaceted, therefore complexity and multifaceted perspectives are needed to guide actions within it'. Our aim in this chapter was to raise some debate about the gendered practices that occur in early childhood settings and to reflect upon how educators can consider boys and girls simultaneously (Browne, 2004). We believe as researchers we are committed to 'tell it how it is' for the children, girls and boys, to convey their 'gendered' (classed and racialised) stories. The poverty of space that is common to many primary school settings in the UK is, we believe, in direct conflict with the ways in which many boys express physicality as part of their play.

Finally, the highly gendered nature of the children's role-play became the variable in which our identities as researchers, sociologists, teachers and women were challenged, causing us endless dialogue and, at times, frustration at how best to resolve our theoretical perspectives with the reality of what we observed. Subsequent presentations of our findings from this study and discussions with colleagues in other institutions have only added to our uncertainty about how far and in what ways we should intervene in such play. As we summarise our research findings and conclude this book, a key question we are left to ponder is something that we raised earlier in this chapter: from a pedagogical standpoint, how can early childhood practitioners widen children's gender scripts whilst also allowing for their individual developmental and social needs to be met? Perhaps the answer is to move towards developing a co-constructed pedagogy of play.

Chapter 7

Rethinking role-play in reception classes

The research reported in this book is based on a small-scale ethnographic study of role-play in reception classes. It set out to explore the relationship between role-play and classroom pedagogy within the context of the early childhood curriculum currently operating in England and Wales and the weighty research literature pointing to the significance of role-play in children's early learning and development. Its focus was on the children's perspectives, drawing on data gathered from what they told us and what we observed in their classrooms. Where it was not possible to elicit their views we have tried to see role-play 'through the eyes' of the children by tapping into their own unique knowledge to help us as adults more fully understand their experiences (Mayall, 2000) of being four-year-olds in school. Working in this way presented us with some methodological challenges and, as we outlined in Chapter 3, reflection on these, in particular the viability of being the 'least adult', might usefully inform future research on children's perspectives.

By drawing on different forms of data we identified prominent themes and issues and described just some of the ways in which young children and their teachers make sense of and experience role-play in the classroom. Though we have drawn liberally on the project data, we have not presented a comprehensive picture of role-play. Rather we have focused on the aspects of role-play in the project reception classes that seemed most pertinent and relevant at that time. As the project was originally conceived, we did not foreground the issue of gender in quite the way it subsequently emerged, nor that understanding its place in children's role-play would prove to be as challenging as it was to us as researchers.

The overall picture we have of role-play in our project classrooms is of an activity valued highly by adults and enjoyed by most, if not all, children. We observed many examples of sustained and highly imaginative play between children, and examples of innovative and creative practice on the part of adults. These observations, however, need to be set against the very real difficulties that reception class teachers face in developing a pedagogy of play that has equal status to the more formal learning required in Key Stage 1.

We want to emphasise that each one of our teachers was a highly skilled and reflective practitioner and that they did all they could in their individual circumstances to overcome pressures from beyond the classroom to prepare children for what was to come in Key Stage 1, particularly in the areas of literacy and numeracy.

The importance of peer culture

This research affirms the widely held view that role-play offers children the means to act out their experiences in a safe environment. It provides a 'space' in which they can escape the 'adult gaze' (Mooney and Blackburn, 2003) and achieve the 'evolution of peer culture' described by Corsaro (1997) among others. Broadhead (2004) suggests it is 'only when we start to see something of the complexity of children's play that we really begin to understand the vastness of their learning' (127). Our own observations bear this out.

Studying role-play from the children's perspective provided insights not simply into the activity and its generic characteristics, but also into important aspects of how young children make sense of early school experience, of 'becoming a pupil', and of navigating classroom rules and routines. Relationships with both peers and adults were central to this. Regular and sustained observation enabled us to see children negotiate, share experiences and interests, and interact with each other in ways that were not possible in other classroom activities. The children deliberately used role-play opportunities to be with friends and sustain their peer culture. In this sense, role-play offered a positive conduit for children to be together in informal and relaxed situations where they could exercise their social, linguistic and imaginative capacities. Thus a leading function of the role-play we observed appeared to be for social interaction between children.

The actual thematic content of the play (for example, playing the customer in the shop) appeared to be of less interest to the children than the opportunity to play with and talk to other children. Several of the examples we have seen illustrate how the children interpreted particular themes and props and then constructed their own stories and narratives. The data also point to the complexities of young children's behaviour in relation to the wider social structures in which they operate, e.g. school, peer groups and with adults. Indeed, it is possible to argue that the class dynamic revolved around the twin poles of peer culture on the one hand and adults on the other. Many of the children we spoke to were clear about what it meant to pretend and more importantly how it felt to be 'in role'. It was something they enjoyed and about which they felt excited. The context of shared pretence in turn sustained children's relationships with one another, providing a frame of reference for exploring and experiencing familiar ideas in unfamiliar ways.

The importance of choice

The concept of choice is ubiquitous in early childhood discourse. Yet in practice, choice is neither a straightforward concept nor one that can be assumed to exist even in apparently child-centred classrooms. Several authors point out that the routines which allow children to be with their friends are largely determined by adults (Broadhead, 2004; Rogers, 2000; Trawick-Smith, 1997). In this study, the grouping of children was often determined by adults according to the perceived learning needs of children. Choice of playmates was for the children an important factor in determining the level of enjoyment and success of the play. Often children would want to continue a game from the previous day or session and, as we have seen, their recall of play events with particular friends was often strong. Our data suggest that for children, choice is an important factor in whether or not they perceive an activity to be play or 'for learning'. Role-play activity was only regarded by children as play when they could choose with whom they played, and had some measure of control over where, how and what they played.

Playing the game

The children made concerted efforts to gain control over their play and, far from being passive recipients, new to school and willing to conform to the decisions made on their behalf by the adults in the classroom, they actively engaged in reconstructing and reinventing the activity even when their actions contradicted or challenged the class routines and the expectations of adults. Where children were routinely pulled away from role-play by adults to undertake other tasks, the play could not easily be revived. As we described in Chapter 5, this was the single most disruptive factor in the quality of play outcomes observed and was often a source of frustration and even subversion for some children. Such was the determination of some children to complete a game or pursue a friendship in their play that they were prepared to resist (and risk conflict with adults), modify the classroom environment, or offer creative alternatives to adult requests. What appear to adults as minor interruptions can have a significant impact on children's play. 'Playing the game' in this way was integral to preserving peer culture within play, to finding ways to realise play interests and goals, and was for the children a way of sustaining and developing their play in the face of adult interests and goals.

Role-play and gender

Much has been made in the literature about the gendered nature of children's role-play and how best practitioners might address the issue (see for example Browne, 2004; Skelton and Hall, 2001). Studies suggest that by the age of four, children already have a firm understanding of the social worlds in which they live: they are classed, raced and gendered (Skeggs, 1997). The issues surrounding the 'gendered' aspects of children's role-play are both complex and challenging. We suggested that too much emphasis on the gendered aspects of children's role-play, and in particular the roles and themes selected, may lead to a rather narrow interpretation of other important aspects of the activity that may have greater personal meaning for the children involved. The complex web of roles and experiences that has already been woven by the time children enter the classroom requires adults to think carefully about how children's gender scripts can be explored and, where appropriate, widened. At the same time key questions have arisen in the course of the research, particularly with regards to the adult role. For example, how might 'barriers' be overcome to ensure children can explore, discover and play with toys and objects that are placed outside their gender positioning? Should adults intervene directly to ensure that all children engage with wider themes, or should children explore and experiment with their own notions of gender through play, even when this means that they adopt normative gender-specific roles? If we take a gender-relational position from which we view children as active participants in developing their gender identities, then the role of the adult is, arguably, to help young children to understand and question conventional gender stereotypes. How, then, do we balance this responsibility against the benefits of role-play, which enables children to interact, communicate with one another and exercise their social skills and imaginations? Adult interventions to 'move children on' from gender-stereotypical play might be counter-productive and inhibit the development of play narratives. Thus from the point of view of children's social development, involvement, engagement and persistence, it can be argued that these episodes were of educational value. We suggest that listening to the children in group activities and through dialogue will open up opportunities to gain valuable information about how they view themselves in role, and what roles appeal to them in their play. As Skelton (2001: 173) suggests, 'children are not too young to think about their own position – of what they see, hear, read, think, say and act out'. Creating opportunities to engage children in dialogue may not change the persistent themes of their play, but it will enable adults to find meaningful and effective ways to widen children's discourses around gender. Many of the most heavily gendered play episodes involved complex social interactions between children and were sustained over long periods. As Campbell *et al.* (2004: 85) remind us: '[We need] to seek multiple perspectives to inform our reading of classroom praxis and in doing so to seek complex and diverse ways to understand and practise with equity intent in early childhood classrooms'.

Role-play from the children's perspective

The case for some kind of reconceptualisation of space and organisation in the reception class seems overwhelming, seen from the children's perspective. It is clear that role-play is valued highly by both children and adults and that it can, if the conditions are right, make a significant contribution to the development of young children. However, in our experience the intervention of certain persistent pedagogical practices often prevents children from realising its potential. Moreover, our findings reinforce the view that in spite of major developments in early childhood education at the level of curriculum and policy, reception classes have not as yet been adequately theorised or conceptualised in ways that determine the most appropriate provision for children aged four and five. This in turn adds to the challenges and dilemmas that reception class practitioners face daily in their work. Evidence from our study reflects other findings, such as research reported by Adams *et al.* (2004). Although change is occurring across the early years sector and there are new ways of working with children and their families in children's centres, plus a reformed foundation stage that purports to focus on the learning needs of reception-class children too, we believe that unless substantial changes are made to the nature of many of these settings in terms of the ways in which they are conceptualised and subsequently organised, changes will not be realised at the level of practice. The general picture to emerge from studies of reception classes, including our own, is one of inconsistency and a continued dichotomy between play and work, between adults' and children's culture in the classroom. Utilising play in relation to a broader interpretation of children's intellectual and social development, as Katz (1999) also suggests, rather than attempting to make it fit narrowly prescribed educational agendas, may be the most satisfactory means by which to resolve such divisions.

Researching young children's perspectives on role-play proved to be both challenging and informative for us. Young children do not always have the tools and the language to express themselves as clearly as researchers or, for that matter, teachers might wish. However, adopting a multi-method, child-focused approach, which included different forms of representation such as drawings and photographs, enabled the children to articulate their views more fully. Listening to the children on multiple levels (Clark and Moss, 2001) yielded important insights into how they were making sense of their experiences. We suggest that by creating opportunities to listen to young children's views about aspects of pedagogy, rather than focusing exclusively on the curriculum and the learning that might arise from it, we may be in a better position to make changes to learning environments and to the ways in which we organise and present play in the classroom. In turn, this might lead to alternative pedagogical approaches that take account of children's active involvement in the development of classroom pedagogy. We suggest, then, that a pedagogy of play might draw not only on adult perspectives of play in school, but on those of the children too. Drawing both on children's responses to and perspectives on the provision of role-play would lead to a genuinely co-constructed (rather than simply reconstructed) pedagogy of play and, we believe, to sustained and more personally meaningful experiences for the children.

In summary, we suggest that the following factors may help us to rethink role-play in reception classes:

- Extended periods of *uninterrupted* role-play would enable children to develop and demonstrate the sustained and complex narratives possible in this age range.
- Listening to children's views about play preferences, use of space and lay-out of the learning environment will raise the value of play in the curriculum and reduce potential tensions between adult and child agendas.
- A more critical reflection on the parameters of 'choice' available within settings is needed.
- Greater recognition of the complexity of role-play for this age group is needed to avoid narrow interpretations of its content and contribution to learning in the Foundation Stage (see also Broadhead, 2004).
- Role-play benefits from styles of adult intervention that extend and rejuvenate play, rather than constrain and frustrate it.
- The use of observation is an effective tool for assessment and a way of auditing children's responses to role-play provision. This presupposes that teachers are available to observe rather than simply to teach while children play.
- Creative and flexible use of space indoors, which challenges the traditional balance between formal, table-top activities and active play-based activities, and that is more in keeping with the Foundation Stage (as opposed to primary school) ethos, would benefit the quality of play in reception classes, particularly for boys.
- Outdoor play encourages children to create play spaces for themselves and to exercise greater choice over materials, location and playmates. Girls appear to take on more active roles and boys appear less disruptive to those around them and may experience fewer instances of conflict with adults.
- Role-play can create opportunities for children and adults to engage in dialogue about gender roles.

Towards a new pedagogy of play?

In a systematic review of early childhood theory and practice the proposal was made that the field might look towards developing a 'new pedagogy of play' (David, 2003). The relationship between play and pedagogy has been a persistent theme throughout this book, although the point was also made in Chapter 1 that the coupling of these concepts is in many ways problematic. This takes us back to the opening of Chapter 2 and to Jessica's imaginary world. At that point we asked: *what kind of pedagogy enables Jessica to initiate such imaginary encounters?* A critical factor in Jessica's classroom was the emphasis on what learners do rather than on what teachers do (Moore, 2004: 170). Clearly teachers and teaching are vitally important. But, as Moore argues in his analysis of what makes a good teacher, an over-emphasis on what teachers do 'can make us lose sight of what – and who – education is really for' (ibid.). As Moore goes on to argue, teachers are faced with 'that rather difficult pedagogic trick of helping young children to achieve academic and creative success *and* to develop as critical, independent and socially responsible citizens' (ibid., original emphasis).

Our own view is that in early childhood classrooms, role-play offers a particularly powerful context for developing pedagogy *with*, rather than separately from, children. First, for children aged three to five, the principal reason for participating in role-play is to be with people you like and are interested in. This alone signals the roots of citizenship and community, which in turn contribute to classrooms as learning communities (Carnell and Lodge, 2002). Second, the imaginative dimension seen in even the most typical examples of role-play is a highly creative act requiring the integration of a network of sophisticated skills acquired in the first few years of life. Third, in role-play we can observe at first hand children's knowledge, values and attitudes about how they are positioned in relation to others by their gender, ethnicity and culture. Thus role-play is one way towards developing pedagogies that are 'genuinely geared towards an uncertain, intriguing, yet-to-be constructed future ... that prioritize the child rather than the curriculum, and that are more concerned with the creation of democratic, culturally inclusive classrooms, than with cultural and behavioural conformity' (Moore, 2004: 171).

Approaches that recognise children's agency and active involvement in making pedagogy seem especially apt in thinking about play. An appropriate curriculum is co-constructed between adults and more knowledgeable others (peers and adults). What we are suggesting is that a pedagogy of play should be co-constructed in this way. In other words, children and adults work together through dialogue, and through adults listening on many levels to how children are finding and making meaning in early childhood settings. But we suggest that a new pedagogy of play might also draw not only on practitioners' and researchers' perspectives of play, but on those of the children too.

Drawing on the work of Anna Craft and her colleagues, we have found the distinction between teaching creatively and teaching for creativity useful in helping to reconfigure current available models of pedagogy as they relate to play. Traditionally in early childhood we have talked of learning through play and more recently teaching through play (Bennett *et al.*, 1997). However, it may be possible to think differently if, following Craft, we adopt the stance of teaching *for* play. This would mean that play would not only be used as a vehicle through which to meet certain curriculum objectives, although that is one possible outcome. Rather children would have a role in shaping the ways in which play is presented in the classroom, through dialogue and activities designed to elicit their views about pedagogical strategies. Craft reports a study of practice in a sixth-form context, where teaching for creativity is highly successful (2005: 45). The study undertaken by Jeffrey *et al.* (cited in Craft, 2005: 45) identified that 'an inclusive approach to pedagogy, where students are welcomed to co-participate with their peers and co-create with their teachers' contributed to this success. Though not related specifically to young children, the principle of a 'learner-inclusive pedagogy' is one that could be developed in early childhood settings and in line with a foundation stage ethos, first to help ameliorate the divisions between play and work, and second to develop a genuinely co-constructed pedagogy of play.

So where does this leave us? Within the reception class as it is currently conceived in many quarters, the contribution of role-play to early learning is subject to a range of external structural and managerial factors such as down-ward pressure (real and perceived) to prepare children for Key Stage 1, lack of good quality outdoor play facilities, over-prescription of role-play areas, and a 'poverty of space' for a genuinely active play-based curriculum. This is partly due to a history of fragmentation in early childhood services in the UK and the lack of 'joined-up' thinking between the various agencies that have a vested interest in children aged four and five; the so-called 'muddle in the middle' (Gelder and Savage, 2004).

The project reported in this book has highlighted some of the complexities of children's play in school and the need for a more extended critique of its role as a vehicle for curriculum delivery within traditional models of class-room pedagogy. Definitions of pedagogy are defined principally from the adults' perspective with little reference to how children respond to and make sense of pedagogical practices. In this way pedagogy may become oppressive, rather than encouraging, and consequently may create unwarranted and energy-wasting resistance in children's play. Drawing play into the heart of pedagogical practice, so that it becomes a space for negotiating cultural val-ues and interests, evaluates questions of voice and power (Giroux, 1994: p.31) and may make more visible the less educationally palatable aspects of play, such as children's interest in popular culture (see also Marsh, 2000), gun play (see Holland, 2003) and gender-stereotypical behaviours and attitudes (MacNaughton, 2000; Browne, 2004). Adopting a co-constructed pedagogy of play that incorporates a critical standpoint on the part of practitioners also has the potential to provide a powerful context for exploring identities, social justice and cultural diversity (see also Brooker, 2002). Sharing of power between adults and children in the teaching and learning context is especially apt in play given its child-led quality; thus we argue here that a co-constructed pedagogy of play may facilitate children's participation further in how their play manifests itself in classrooms. We propose also that co-constructing a pedagogy of play requires children to be involved in the decision-making processes that surround play provision. This would involve listening to children on multiple levels. We envisage that talking about and recording in different forms how children are making sense of the play environment, rather than focusing on learning outcomes, would contribute to practitioners' assessments of how children are learning. Further, to look at the pedagogical practices that operate in children's 'spaces' (or, put another way, to explore children's relationships with their institutions) would enable practitioners to explore how they construct identities, values and knowledge with others, and would foster pedagogical approaches that take us 'beyond listening' (Clark et al., 2005). Working in this way would open up arenas for stronger equity practices and offer alternatives to the adoption of zero tolerance approaches that outlaw, for example, gun play and Barbies – as we have seen in Chapters 5 and 6 this does little more than subvert the play. Many of these ideas are shared by our colleagues in the early childhood community; however, current practices in the UK educational context perpetuate the traditional dichotomies between play and work, children's culture/adults' culture, and adult intensive and child initiated. Play and especially role-play would, we believe, provide an ideal site for opening up a space for young children and adults to exchange meaning and share cultural perspectives. Sharing of power between adults and children in the teaching and learning context is especially apt in play; thus we argue here that a co-constructed pedagogy of play may facilitate children's further participation in how their play manifests itself in classrooms.

Glossary

Curriculum Guidance for the Foundation Stage (CGFS)

A curriculum framework for children aged three to five years, introduced in England and Wales in 2000. It comprises six areas of learning: personal, social and emotional development; communication, language and literacy; mathematical development; knowledge and understanding of the world; physical development; and creative development.

Early Years Foundation Stage (EYFS)

Due to be implemented in 2008 to supersede the CGFS, a curriculum framework for children aged from birth to five years in England and Wales.

Education Reform Act 1988 (ERA)

The first major reform of education in England and Wales since 1944, it included the introduction of the National Curriculum.

Key Stages

There are four stages of the National Curriculum: Key Stage 1 for pupils aged five to seven years; Key Stage 2 for pupils aged seven to eleven; Key Stage 3 for pupils aged eleven to fourteen; Key Stage 4 for pupils aged fourteen to sixteen.

National Curriculum (NC)

Introduced in 1988 for children of statutory school age (five to sixteen years) in England and Wales, it sets out the subjects and concepts that should be taught. The NC comprises ten subjects, of which English, maths and science are core.

Local Authorities (LAs)

Local government departments with responsibility for the coordination and administration of local services, including education.

Office for Standards in Education (Ofsted)

The body that is charged with the task of inspecting state-maintained early childhood settings, schools and colleges in England and Wales.

Plowden Report

A report on primary education led by Lady Plowden entitled *Children and their Primary Schools* and published in 1967. It emphasised in particular the importance of child-centred education, learning through play and parental involvement in children's schooling. Its influence on policy and practice is widely acknowledged.

Qualifications and Curriculum Authority (QCA)

Sponsored by the Department for Education and Skills (DfES), the QCA is the official body that regulates, develops and modernises the curriculum, assessments, examinations and qualifications in the UK.

Standard Assessment Tasks (SATs)

At the end of each Key Stage of the National Curriculum children are assessed by their teacher. In addition, at the end of Key Stages 2, 3 and 4, children are also subject to national tests to determine both their progress through the National Curriculum and the individual school's performance.

References

Adams, S., Alexander, E., Drummond, M.J. and Moyles, J. (2004) *Inside the Foundation Stage: Recreating the Reception Year*, London: ATL.

Alderson, P. (1995) *Listening to Children: Children, Ethics and Social Research*, London: Barnardos.

Andreson, H. (2005) 'Role play and language development in the preschool years', *Culture and Pedagogy*, 11 (4): 387–414.

Anning, A. (2004) 'The Co-construction of an Early Childhood Curriculum'. In Anning, A., Cullen, J. and Fleer, M. (eds), *Early Childhood Education Society and Culture*, London: Sage Publications Ltd.

Anning, A. (2006) 'Early years education: mixed messages and conflicts', in D. Kassem, E. Mufti J. Robinson (eds), *Education Studies: Issues and Critical Perspectives*, 5–17.

Archard, D. (1993) *Children: Rights and Childhood*, London: Routledge.

Arnot, M. (2002) *Reproducing Gender? Essays on Educational Theory and Feminist Politics*, London: RoutledgeFalmer.

Atkin, J. (1991) 'Thinking about play', in N. Hall and L. Abbott (eds), *Play in the Primary Curriculum*, London: Hodder and Stoughton.

Aubrey, C. (2004) 'Implementing the foundation stage in reception classes', *British Educational Research Journal*, 30 (5): 633–656.

Aubrey, C. with Taylor Nelson Sofres (2002) *Implementing The Foundation Stage in Reception Class*, DfES Research Brief 350. Available at: www.dfes.gov.uk/research/data/uploadfiles/RB350.pdf.

Avgitidou, S. (1994) 'Children's friendships in early schooling: cross cultural and educational case studies', unpublished PhD thesis, University of Sussex.

Avgitidou, S. (1997) 'Children's play: an investigation of children's co-construction of their world within early school settings', *Early Years*, 17 (2) Spring: 6–10.

Bailey, R. (2002) 'Playing social chess – social play and social intelligence', *Early Years*, 22 (2): 163–173.

Bailey, R. and Farrow, S. (1998) 'Play and problem-solving in a new light', *International Journal of Early Years Education*, 6 (3): 265–275.

Baillargeon, R. (1987) 'Object permanence in 3.5- and 4.5-month-old infants', *Developmental Psychology*, 23: 655–664.

Baldock, P. (2006) *The Place of Narrative in the Early Years Curriculum: How the Tale Unfolds*, London: Routledge.

Baldock, P., Fitzgerald, D. and Kay, J. (2005) *Understanding Early Years Policy*, London: Paul Chapman.

Ball, S.J. (1998) 'Performativity and fragmentation in "postmodern schooling"', in J. Carter (ed.) *Postmodernity and the Fragmentation of Welfare*, London: Routledge.

Baron-Cohen, S. (2003) *The Essential Difference*, London: Penguin.

Bateson, G. (1973) *Steps to an Ecology of Mind*, London: Paladin.

Baxter, J. (2001) *Making Gender Work*, Reading: Reading and Language Information Centre.

Beardsley, G. and Harnett, P. (1998) *Exploring Play in the Primary School*, London: David Fulton.

Bennett, N. and Kell, J. (1989) *A Good Start? Four-Year-Olds in Infant Schools*, London: Blackwell.

Bennett, N., Wood, L. and Rogers, S. (1997) *Teaching through Play: Teachers' Thinking and Classroom Practice*, Buckingham: Open University Press.

Bergen, D. (2002) 'The role of play in children's cognitive development', *Early Childhood Research and Practice*, 4 (1). Available at: http://ecrp.uiuc.edu/v4nl/bergen.html (last accessed 1 June 2007).

Bergstrom, M. and Ikonen, P. (2005) 'Space to play, room to grow', *Children in Scotland*, April: 12–13.

Bhatti, G. (1999) *Asian Children at Home and at School: An Ethnographic Study*, London: Routledge.

Bilton, H. (1997) *Outdoor Play: Management and Innovation*, London: David Fulton.

Blaise, M. (2005) *Playing it Straight: Uncovering Gender Discourses in the Early Childhood Classroom*, London: Routledge.

Blatchford, P., Kutnick, P., Baines, E. and Galton, M. (2003) 'Towards a social pedagogy of classroom group work', *International Journal of Educational Research, 39*: 153–172.

Bloch, M.N. and Pellegrini, A.D. (1989) Ways of looking at children, context and play. In Bloch, M.N. and Pellegrini, A.D. (eds), *The Ecological Context of Children's Play*, Norwood, New Jersey: Ablex Publishing Corporation.

Broadhead, P. (2004) *Early Years Play and Learning*, London: RoutledgeFalmer.

Brogstrom, S. (1997) Children's play: tools, symbols and frame play, *Early Years*, 17: 2, 16–21.

Bronfenbrenner, U. (1979) *The Ecology of Human Development*, Cambridge, MA: Harvard University Press.

Brooker, L. (2001) 'Interviewing children', in G. MacNaughton, S.A. Rolfe and I. Siraj-Blatchford (eds), *Doing Early Childhood Research: International Perspectives on Theory and Practice*, 162–177, St Leonards, NSW: Allen and Unwin.

Brooker, L. (2002) *Starting School – Young Children Learning Cultures*, Buckingham: Open University Press.

Brooker, L. (2006) 'From home to the home corner: observing children's identity-maintenance in early childhood settings', *Children and Society*, 20 (2): 116–127.

Browne, N. (2004) *Gender Equity in the Early Years*, Buckingham: Open University Press.

Browne, N. and Ross, C. (1991) 'Girls' stuff, boys' stuff: young children talking and playing', in N. Browne (ed.), *Science and Technology in the Early Years: An Equal Opportunities Approach*, Buckingham: Open University Press.

Bruce, T. (1989) *Early Childhood Education*, London: Hodder and Stoughton.

Bruce, T. (1991) *Time to Play*, London: Hodder and Stoughton.

Bruce, T. (1996) *Helping Young Children to Play*, London: Hodder Arnold.

Buckingham, D. (2003) *Media Education: Literacy, Learning and Contemporary Culture*, Cambridge: Polity.

Burman, E. (1994) *Deconstructing Developmental Psychology*, London: Routledge.

CACE (Central Advisory Council for Education) (1967) *Children and their Primary Schools* (Plowden Report), London: HMSO.

Campbell, S., MacNaughton, G., Page, J. and Rolfe, S. (2004) 'Beyond quality, advancing social justice and equity: interdisciplinary explorations of working for equity and social justice in early childhood education', in S. Reifel and M. Brown (eds), *Social Contexts of Early Education and Reconceptualizing Play (II). Advances in Early Education and Day Care*, 13, 55–91, Elsevier.

Carnell, E. and Lodge, C. (2002) *Supporting Effective Learning*, London: Paul Chapman.

Carpendale, J. and Lewis, C. (2006) *How Children Develop Social Understanding*, Oxford: Blackwell.

Christensen, P. (2004) 'Children's participation in ethnographic research: issues of power and representation', *Children and Society*, 18: 165–176.

Christensen, P. and James, A. (eds) (2000) *Research with Children: Perspectives and Practices*, London: Falmer.

Christensen, P. and James, A. (2002) 'What are schools for? The temporal experience of children's learning in Northern England', in R. Edwards (ed.), *Children, Home and School: Regulation, Autonomy or Correction?* London: RoutledgeFalmer.

Chung, S. and Walsh, D.J. (2000) 'Unpacking child-centredness: a history of meanings', *Journal of Curriculum Studies*, 32 (2) March: 215–234.

Clark, A. and Moss, P. (2001) *Listening to Young Children: The Mosaic Approach*, London: NCB.

Clark, A., Kjørholt, A.T. and Moss, P. (2005) *Beyond Listening: Children's Perspectives on Early Childhood Services*, Bristol: Policy.

Cleave, S. and Brown, S. (1991) *Early to School: Four Year Olds in Infant Classes*, London: NFER/Routledge.

Cohen, D. (1993) *The Development of Play*, 2nd edn, London: Croom Helm.

Cole, M. (1996) *Cultural Psychology: A Once and Future Discipline*, Harvard: Belknap Press of Harvard University Press.

Connell, R. (1987) *Gender and Power: Society, the Person and Sexual Politics*, Cambridge: Blackwell.

Connolly, P. (2006) '"The masculine habitus as distributed cognition": a case study of 5–6-year-old boys in an English inner city multi-ethnic primary school', *Children and Society*, 20 (2) April: 140–152.

Cooper, N. and Stevenson, C. (1997) 'Qualitative and Quantitative Research.', *The Psychologist*, 10 (4): 159–162.

Corsaro, W.A. (1985) *Friendship and Peer Culture in the Early Years*, Norwood, NJ: Ablex.

Corsaro, W.A. (1997) *The Sociology of Childhood*, London: Pine Forge.

Corsaro, W.A. (2005) *The Sociology of Childhood*, 2nd edn, London: Pine Forge.

Craft, A. (2005) *Creativity in Schools*, London: Routledge.

Critcher, C. (2003) *Moral Panics and the Media*, Buckingham: Open University Press.

Csikszentmihalyi, M. (1981) 'Play, paradigm and paradox', in A.T. Cheska (ed.), *Play as Context*, New York: Leisure.

Daniels, H. (1993) 'The individual and the organisation', in Daniels, H. (ed.), *Charting the agenda: educational activity after Vygotsky*, London: Paul Chapman.

Daniels, S., Redfern, E. and Shorrocks-Taylor, D. (1995) 'Trends in the early admission of children to school: appropriate or expedient?' *Educational Research*, 37 (3): 239–249.

Daniels, S., Shorrocks-Taylor, D. and Redfern, E (2000) 'Can starting summer-born children earlier at infant school improve their National Curriculum results?' *Oxford Review of Education*, 26 (2): 207–220.

Darling, J. (1994) *Child-centred Education and its Critics*, London: Paul Chapman.

David, T. (1990) *Under Five – Under-Educated?* Milton Keynes: Open University Press.

David, T. (2003) *What do we Know about Teaching Young Children? A Professional User Review of UK research based on the BERA Academic Review 'Early Years Research: Pedagogy, Curriculum and Adult Roles, Training and Professionalism'*, Canterbury: Canterbury Christ Church University College.

Davies, B. (1989) *Frogs and Snails and Feminist Tales: Preschool Children and Gender*, Sydney: Allen and Unwin.

Davis, J. (1998) 'Understanding the meanings of children: a reflexive process', *Children and Society*, 12 (5): 325–335.

DES (Department of Education and Science) (1989) *Aspects of Primary Education: The Education of Children under Five*, London: HMSO.

DES (Department of Education and Science) (1990) *Starting with Quality: Report of Committee of Inquiry into the Quality of the Educational Experience Offered to Three and Four Year Olds* (Rumbold Report), London: DES.

de Vaus, D. (1996) *Surveys in Social Research*, London: UCL.

Devine, D. (2003) *Children, Power and Schooling: How Childhood is Structured in the Primary School*, Stoke-on-Trent: Trentham.

DfES (Department for Education and Skills) (2003) *Excellence and Enjoyment: Strategy for Primary Schools*, Notts: DfES publications.

DfES (Department for Education and Skills) (2007) *The Early Years Foundation Stage: Setting the Standards for Learning Development and Care in Children from Birth to Five*. Available at: http://www.standards.dfes.gov.uk/eyfs/ (accessed 8 June 2007).

Donaldson, M. (1978) *Children's Minds*, London: Fontana.

Drummond, M.J. (2005) 'Professional amnesia: a suitable case for treatment', *Forum*, 47 (2/3): 83–90.

Dunn, J. (2004) *Children's Friendships*, Oxford: Blackwell.

Dunn, J. (2005) 'Naturalistic observations of children and their families', in S. Greene and D. Hogan (eds), *Researching Children's Experiences: Approaches and Methods*, London: Sage.

Epstein, D., Elwood, J., Hey, V. and Maw, J. (2002) *Failing Boys?: Issues in Gender and Achievement*, Buckingham: Oxford University Press.

Erikson, E. (1963) *Childhood and society*, New York: Norton & Co.

Evans, P. and Fuller, M. (1998) 'Children's perceptions of their nursery education', *International Journal of Early Years Education*, 6 (1): 59–74.

Fisher, J. (1996) *Starting from the Child*, Buckingham: Oxford University Press.

Fisher, J. (2001) *Starting from the Child*, 2nd edn, Buckingham: Oxford University Press.

Fisher, R. (2000) 'Developmentally appropriate practice and a National Literacy Strategy', *British Journal of Educational Studies*, 48 (1): 58–69.

Frost, J., Shin, D. and Jacobs, P. (1998) 'Physical environments and children's play', in O. Saracho and B. Spodek (eds), *Multiple Perspectives on Play in Early Childhood Education*, Albany, NY: State University of New York Press.

Garbarino, J. (1989) 'An ecological perspective on the role of play in development', in M. Bloch and A. Pellegrini (eds), *The Ecological Context of Children's Play*, Norwood, NJ: Ablex.

Garrick, R. (2004) *Playing Outdoors in the Early Years*, London: Continuum.

Garvey, C. (1990) *Play*, 2nd edn, London: Fontana.

Gelder, U. and Savage, J. (2004) 'Children and social policy: a case study of four-year-olds in school', in J. Willan, R. Parker-Rees and J. Savage (eds), *Early Childhood Studies*, Exeter: Learning Matters.

Giroux, H. (1994) *Disturbing Pleasures*, New York: Routledge.

Gopnik, A., Meltzoff, A. and Kuhl, P. (1999) *How Babies Think: The Science of Childhood*, London: Wiedenfeld and Nicolson.

Guha, M. (1988) 'Play in school', in G.M. Blenkin and A.V. Kelly (eds), *Early Childhood Education: A Developmental Curriculum*, London: Paul Chapman.

Guss, F. (2004) 'Reconceptualizing play: aesthetic self-definitions', *Contemporary Issues in Early Childhood*, 6 (3): 233-243.

Guss, F. (2005) 'Dramatic playing beyond the theory of multiple intelligences', *Research in Drama Education*, 10 (1): 43-54.

Hall, N. (1994) 'Play, literacy and the role of the teacher', in J. Moyles (ed.), *The Excellence of Play*, Buckingham: Open University Press.

Hall, N. and Abbott, L. (1991) *Play in the Primary Curriculum*, London: Hodder and Stoughton.

Hammersley, M. and Atkinson, P. (1995) *Ethnography: Principles in Practice*, London: Routledge.

Hammersley, M. and Atkinson, P. (2006) *Ethnography: Principles in Practice*, 2nd edn, London: Routledge.

Hannikainen, M. (1995) 'Young children's role play in a day care context: a Vygotskian perspective', paper presented at the European Conference on Educational Research, Bath.

Harden, J., Scott, S., Backett-Milburn, K. and Jackson, S. (2000) 'Can't talk won't talk?: Methodological issues in researching children', *Sociological Research Online*. Available at: http://www.socresonline.org.uk/5/2/harden.html.

Harris, P. (2000) *The Work of the Imagination*, Oxford: Blackwell.

Hartup, W.W., French, D.C., Laursen, B., Johnston, M.K. and Ogawa, J.R. (1993) 'Conflict and friendship relations in middle childhood: behaviour in a closed field setting', *Child Development*, 64, 445–454.

Hill, M., Davis, J., Prout, A. and Tisdall, K. (2004) 'Moving the participation agenda forward', *Children and Society*, 18 (2): 77–96.

Hill, M., Laybourn, A. and Borland, M. (1996) 'Engaging with primary-aged children about their emotions and well-being: methodological considerations', *Children and Society*, 10 (2): 129–144.

Hobson, P. (2002) *The Cradle of Thought: Exploring the Origins of Thinking*, Basingstoke: MacMillan.

Holland, P. (1999) 'Just pretending', *Language Matters*, (Spring): 1–5, Centre for Language in Primary Education.

Holland, P. (2000) 'Take the toys from the boys? An examination of the genesis and appropriateness of adult perspectives in the area of war, weapon and superhero play', *Children's Social and Economics Education*, 4 (2): 92–108.

Holland, P. (2003) *We Don't Play with Guns Here: War, Weapons and Superhero Play in The Early Years*, Maidenhead: Open University Press.

Hood, S., Kelley, P. and Mayall, B. (1996) 'Children as research subjects: a risky enterprise', *Children and Society*, 10 (2): 117–128.

Howard, J., Bellin, W. and Rees, V. (2001) 'Eliciting children's perceptions of play and exploiting playfulness to maximise learning in the early years classroom', paper presented at the Annual Conference of the British Educational Research Association, University of Exeter, England, 12–14 September 2002.

Hutt, S.J., Tyler, S., Hutt, C. and Christopherson, H. (1989) *Play, Exploration and Learning: A Natural History of the Pre-school*, London: Routledge.

Isaacs, S. (1929) *The Nursery Years: The Mind of the Child from Birth to Six*, London: Routledge and Kegan Paul.

Isaacs, S. (1933) *Social Development in Young Children*, London: Routledge and Kegan Paul.

Isenberg, J.P. and Quisenberry, N. (2002) 'Play: essential for all children', *Childhood Education*, 79 (1): 33–39.

James, A. (1999) *Changing Childhood, Changing Children*, paper presented at the Mind The Gap Conference, University of Leicester (September).

James, A. Jenks, C. and Prout, A. (1998) *Theorising Childhood*, Oxford: Polity.

Jenkins, J. and Astington, J. (2000) 'Theory of mind and social behaviour: causal models tested in a longitudinal study', *Merrill-Palmer Quarterly*, 46 (3): 203–220.

Jenkinson, S. (2001) *The Genius of Play: Celebrating the Spirit of Childhood*, Stroud: Hawthorn.

Jenks, C. (2000) 'Zeitgeist research on children', in P. Christensen and A. James (eds), *Research with Children: Perspectives and Practices*, London: Falmer.

Johnson, J. (1990) 'The role of play in cognitive development', in E. Klugman and S. Smilansky (eds), *Children's Play and Learning: Perspectives and Policy Implications*, New York: Teachers' College Press.

Jordan, B. (2004) 'Scaffolding learning and co-constructing understandings', in A. Anning, J. Cullen and M. Fleer (eds), *Early Childhood Education: Society and Culture*, London: Sage.

Jordan, E. (1995) 'Fighting boys and fantasy play: the construction of masculinity in the early years of school', *Gender and Education*, 7 (1): 69–86.

Katz, L.G. (1999) 'Another look at what young children should be learning', ERIC Digest.

Kavkler, M., Tancig, S., Magajna, L. and Aubrey, C. (2000) 'Getting it right from the start? The influence of early school entry on later achievements in mathematics', *European Early Childhood Education Research Journal*, 8 (1): 75–93.

Keating, I., Fabian, H., Jordan, P., Mavers, D. and Roberts, J. (2002) '"Well I've not done any work today. I don't know why I came to school." Perceptions of play in the reception class', *Educational Studies*, 26 (4): 437–454.

King, N. (1992) 'The impact of context on children's play in school', in S. Kessler and B. Swadner (eds), *Reconceptualising the Early Childhood Curriculum: Beginning the Dialogue*, New York: Teacher's College Press.

Kitson, N. (1997) 'Adult intervention in children's socio-dramatic play', 2nd edn, *Education*, 3–13.

Laevers, F. (1993) Deep level learning: an exemplary application on the area of physical knowledge. *European Early Childhood Research Journal*, 1: 1, 53–68.

Lansdown, G. (1994) 'Children's rights', in B. Mayall (ed.), *Children's Childhoods: Observed and Experienced*, London: Falmer.

Lather, P. (1995) 'Feminist perspectives on empowering research methodologies', in J. Holland, M. Blair and S. Sheldon (eds), *Debates and Issues in Feminist Research and Pedagogy*, Clevedon: Open University Press.

Leach, J. and Moon, B. (eds) (1999) *Learners and Pedagogy*, London: PCP, with Buckingham: Open University Press.

Macguire, P. (1991) 'Social space: gender inequalities and educational differentiation', *British Journal of the Sociology of Education*, 12 (1).

Maclean, R. (1996) 'Quick! Hide! Constructing a playground identity in the early weeks of school', *Language and Education*, 10: (2/3): 171–186.

McLean, S.V. (1991) *The Human Encounter: Teachers and Children Living Together in Preschools*, London: Falmer.

MacNaughton, G. (2000) *Rethinking Gender in Early Childhood Education*, London: Paul Chapman.

Mahon, A., Glendinning, C., Clarke, K. and Craig, G. (1996) 'Researching children: methods and ethics', *Children and Society*, 10 (2): 145–154.

Mandell, N. (1991) 'The least adult role in studying children', *Studying the Social Worlds of Children*, Basingstoke: Falmer.

Marsh, J. (1999) 'Batman and Batwoman go to school: popular culture in the literacy curriculum', *International Journal of Early Years Education*, 7 (2): 117–131.

Marsh, J. (2000) '"But I want to fly too!": Girls and superhero play in the infant classroom', *Gender and Education*,12 (2): 209–220.

Mayall, B. (1994) *Children's Childhoods: Observed and Experienced*, London: Falmer.

Mayall, B. (1996) *Children, Health and the Social Order*, Buckingham: Open University Press.

Mayall, B. (2000) 'Conversations with children: working with generational issues', in P. Christensen and A. James (eds), *Research with Children: Perspectives and Practices*, London: Falmer.

Meade, A. (2006) *Education Facilities for Young Children*, OECD.

Meadows, S. and Cashdan, A. (1988) *Helping Young Children Learn: Contributions to a Cognitive Curriculum*, London: David Fulton.

Meckley, M. (1996) 'Studying children's social play through a child cultural approach: roles, rules, and shared knowledge', in S. Reifel (ed.), *Social Contexts of Early Development in Education Advances in Early Education and Day Care*, Greenwich, CT: AI Press.

Messner, M. (2000) Barbie girls versus sea monsters: children constructing gender', *Gender and Society*, 14 (6): 765–784.

Millard, E. (1997) *Differently Literate*, London: Falmer.

Mooney, A. and Blackburn, T. (2003) 'Children's views on childcare quality', DfES Research Report RR482, London: HMSO.

Moore, A. (2004) *The Good Teacher: Dominant Discourses in Teaching and Teacher Education*, London: Routledge.

Morgan, D. (1997) *Focus Groups as Qualitative Research*, London: Sage.

Morrow, V. and Richards, M. (1996) 'The ethics of social research with children: an overview', *Children and Society*, 10 (2): 90–105.

Moyles, J. (1989) *Just Playing? The Role and Status of Play in Early Childhood Education*, Buckingham: Open University Press.

Moyles, J. (ed.) (2005) *The Excellence of Play*, Buckingham: Open University Press.

Newman, F. and Holzman, L. (1993) *Lev Vygotsky: Revolutionary Scientist*, London: Routledge.

Newson, J. and Newson, E. (1968) *Four Year Olds in an Urban Environment*, London: Allen and Urwin.

Nichols, S. and Stich, S. (2000) 'A cognitive theory of pretense', *Cognition*, 74 (2): 115–147.

Office for Standards in Education (Ofsted) (1993) *First Class: The Standards and Quality of Education in Reception Classes*, London: HMSO.

Olofsson, B.K. (1991) 'Doing reality with play: play as a children's resource in organizing everyday life in daycare centres', in H. Strandell (ed.), *Childhood: A Global Journal of Child Research*, 4 (4): November.

Paechter, C. (2003) 'Masculinities and femininities as communities of practice', *Women's Studies International Forum*, 26 (1): 69–77.

Pahl, K. (1999) *Transformations: Meaning Making in Nursery Education*, Stoke-on Trent: Trentham.

Paley, V.G. (1984) *Boys and Girls*, Chicago: University of Chicago Press.

Paley, V.G. (1992) *You Can't Say You Can't Play*, Cambridge: Harvard University Press.

Parker-Rees, R. (1999) 'Protecting playfulness', in L. Abbott and H. Moylett (eds), *Early Education Transformed*, 61–72, London: Falmer.

Pascal, C. (1990) *Under-Fives in the Infant Classroom*, Stoke-on-Trent: Trentham.

Pellegrini, A. and Boyd, B. (1993) 'The role of play in early childhood development and education: issues of definition and function', in B. Spodek (ed.), *Handbook of Research on the Education of Young Children*, New York: Macmillan.

Perry, J. (2001) *Outdoor Play: Teaching Strategies with Young Children*, New York: Teacher's College Press.

Petrie, P., Egharevba, I., Oliver, C. and Poland, G. (2000) *Out of School Lives, Out of School Services*, London: Stationery Office.

Piaget, J. (1962) *Play, Dreams and Imitation in Childhood*, New York: Norton.

Pollard, A. (1993) 'Learning in primary schools', in H. Daniels (ed.), *Charting the Agenda: Educational Activity after Vygotsky*, London: Routledge.

Pollard, A. (1996) *The Social World of Children's Learning*, London: Cassell.

Powell, K., Danby, S. and Farrell, A. (2006) 'Investigating an account of children passing: how boys and girls operate differently in relation to an everyday, classroom regulatory practice', *Journal of Early Childhood Research*, 4 (3): 259–275.

Prosser, J. (1998) *Image Based Research*, London: Falmer.

Prout, A. (2000) *Opening Address. Children: Making their future? Research and Policy for the 21st Century*, London (Final Conference ESRC 5–16 research programme).

Prout, A. (2001) 'Representing children: reflections on the children 5–16 programme', *Children and Society*, 15 (3): 913–201.

Prout, A. and James, A. (1997) 'A new paradigm for the sociology of childhood?', in A. James and A. Prout (eds), *Constructing and Reconstructing Childhood*, 7–33, London: Falmer Press.

QCA (2000) *Curriculum Guidance for the Foundation Stage*, London: Department for Education and Employment.

Quicke, J. (1994) 'Learning and context: constructing an integrated perspective', *British Journal of Sociology*, 17 (1): 103.

Qvortrup, J. (1987) 'Introduction to the sociology of childhood', *International Journal of Sociology*, 17 (3): 3–37.

Qvortrup, J. (1994) 'Childhood matters: an introduction', in J. Qvortrup, M. Bardy, G. Sgritta and H. Wintersberger (eds), *Childhood Matters: Social Theory, Practice and Politics*, Brookfrield: Avebury.

Read, J. (2006) 'Free play with Froebel: use and abuse of progressive pedagogy in London's nineteenth century infant schools', *Pedagogica Historica*, 42 (3): 299–323.

Reifel, S. and Brown, M. (eds) (2004) *Social Contexts of Early Education and Reconceptualizing Play II: Advances in Early Education and Day Care*, Vol. 13: 55–91, Oxford, England: Elsevier.

Rich, D. (2003) 'BANG! BANG!: Gun play, and why children need it', *Early Education*, Summer.

Roberts, P. (2006) *Nurturing Creativity in Young People*, DCMS/DfES.

Robinson, K.H. and Jones Díaz, K. (2006) *Diversity and Difference in Early Childhood Education: Issues for Theory and Practice*, London: Open University Press.

Rogers, S. (1998) 'Play: a conflict of interests?' Paper presented at the British Educational Research Association Conference, Belfast, August.

Rogers, S. (2000) 'Play in school: a qualitative study of teacher perspectives', unpublished PhD, University of Reading.

Rogers, S. and Evans, J. (2006) 'Playing the game: children's perspectives of role-play', *European Early Childhood Education Research Journal*, 14 (1): 43–56.

Rogers, S. and Rose, J. (2007) 'Ready for reception? The advantages and disadvantages of single-point entry to school', *Early Years*, 27 (1): March: 47–63.

Rogoff, B. (1990) *Apprenticeship in Thinking: Cognitive Development in Social Context*, New York: Oxford University Press.

Rubin, K.H. (1980) 'Fantasy play: its role in the development of social skills and social cognition', in K.H. Rubin (ed.), *Children's Play*, 69–84, San Francisco: Jossey-Bass.

Rubin, K.H., Fein, G.G. and Vandenberg, B. (1983) 'Play', in E.M. Hetherington (ed.) and P.H. Mussen (series ed.), *Handbook of Child Psychology: Socialization, Personality and Social Development*, Vol. 4, 693–774, New York: Wiley.

Sanders, D., White, G., Burge, B., Sharp, C., Eames, A., McEune, R. and Grayson, H. (2005) *A Study of the Transition from the Foundation Stage to Key Stage 1*, DfES Research Report SSU/2005/FR/013, London: DfES.

Saunders, A. (1989) 'Creativity in the infant classroom', in G. Barrett (ed.), *Disaffection from School? The Early Years*, London: Falmer.

Scales, B. (1996) 'Researching the hidden curriculum', in J. Chafel and S. Reifel (eds), *Advances in Early Education and Day Care: Theory and Practice in Early Childhood Teaching*, Vol. 8, 237–259, Greenwich, CT: JAI Press.

Schwartzman, H.B. (1978) *Transformations: The anthropology of children's play*, New York: Plenum Publishing Corporation.

Sestini, E. (1987) 'The quality of learning experiences for four-year-olds in infant classes', in NFER/SCDC (eds), *Four-Year-Olds in School: Policy and Practice*, Slough: NFER.

Sharp, C. (2002) *School Starting Age: European Policy and Recent Research*, Conference Paper, NFER.

Simon, B. (1991) *Education and the Social Order*, London: Laurence and Wishart.

Singer, J. (1973) *The Child's World of Make-Believe: Experimental Studies of Imaginative Play*, New York: Academic Press.

Siraj-Blatchford, I. and Sylva, K. (2004) 'Researching pedagogy in English pre-schools', *British Educational Research Journal*, 30 (5): 713–730.

Skeggs, B. (1997) *Formations of Class and Gender*, London: Sage.

Skelton, C. (2001) *Schooling the Boys: Masculinities and Primary Education*, Buckingham: Open University Press.

Skelton, C. and Francis, B. (eds) (2003) *Boys and Girls in the Primary Classroom*, Buckingham: Open University Press.

Skelton, C. and Hall, E. (2001) *The Development of Gender Roles in Young Children: A review of policy and literature*, Manchester: Equal Opportunities Commission.

Smilansky, S. (1990) 'Sociodramatic play: its relevance to behaviour and achievement in school', in E. Klugman and S. Smilansky (eds), *Children's Play and Learning: Perspectives and Policy Implications*, New York: Teachers' College Press.

Smilansky, S. and Shefatya, L. (1990) *Facilitating Play*, Silver Spring, MD: Psychological and Educational Publications.

Smith, P.K. (1988) 'Children's play and its role in early development: a re-evaluation of the "play ethos"', in A.D. Pellegini (ed.), *Psychological Bases to Early Childhood Education*, Colchester: John Wiley.

Smith, P.K. (1990) 'The role of play in the nursery and primary curriculum', in C. Rogers and P. Kutnick (eds), *The Social Psychology of the Primary School*, London: Routledge.

Smith, P.K. (2005) 'Physical activity and rough-and-tumble play', in J. Moyles (ed.), *The Excellence of Play*, 127–137, Buckingham: Open University Press.

Staggs, L. (2004) *Common Obstacles and Possible Solutions*, Effective Reception Class Practice Conference, DfES. Available at: http://www.lgfl.net/lgfl/leas/hackney/accounts/staff/foundationlt/web/effective/index/ (accessed 10 May 2006).

Stanley, L. (1990) *Breaking Out: Feminist Consciousness and Feminist Research*, London: Routledge.

Steedman, C. (1987) *The Tidy House: Little Girls Writing*, London: Virago.

Stephenson, A. (1998) 'Opening up the outdoors: a reappraisal of young children's outdoor experiences', unpublished Masters thesis, Victoria University of Wellington.

Stephenson, A. (2002) 'Opening up the outdoors: exploring the relationship between the indoor and outdoor environments of a centre', *European Early Childhood Education Research Journal*, 10 (1): 29–38.

Stevenson, C. (1987) 'Young four-year-olds in nursery and infant classes: challenges and constraints', in NFER/SCDC, *Four Year Olds in School: Policy and Practice*, Slough: NFER/SCDC.

Stone, G. (1971) 'The play of little children', in R.E. Herron and B. Sutton-Smith (eds), *Child's Play*, New York: John Wiley.

Strandell, H. (2000) 'What is the use of children's play: preparation or social particiption?' In H. Penn (ed.), *Early Childhood Services: Theory, Policy and Practice*, Buckingham: Open University Press.

Sugrue, C. (1997) *Complexities of Teaching: Child-centred Perspectives*, London: Falmer.

Sutherland, P. (1992) *Cognitive Development Today: Piaget and his Critics*, London: Paul Chapman.

Sutton-Smith B. (1971) 'The role of play in cognitive development', in R. Herron and B. Sutton-Smith (eds), *Child's Play*, New York: John Wiley.

Sutton-Smith, B. (1995) 'Conclusion: the persuasive rhetorics of play', in A.D. Pellegrini (ed.), *The Future of Play Theory*, New York: State University of New York Press.

Sutton-Smith, B. (1997) *The Ambiguity of Play, Cambridge*, MA: Harvard University Press.

Sutton-Smith, B. and Kelly-Byrne, D. (1984) 'The idealization of play', in P.K.Smith (ed.), *Play in Animals and Humans*, Oxford: Blackwell.

Swain, J. (2004) 'The resources and strategies that 10–11-year-old boys use to construct masculinities in the school setting', *British Educational Research Journal*, 30 (1): 167–185.

Sylva, K., Melhuish, E., Sammons, P., Siraj-Blatchford, I. and Taggart, B. (2004) T*he Effective Provision of Pre-School Education (EPPE) Project: Final Report*, London: Institute of Education.

Sylva, K., Roy, C. and Painter, M. (1980) *Childwatching at Playgroup and Nursery*, London: Grant McIntyre.

Taggart, B. (2004) 'Early years education and care: three agendas', *British Educational Research Journal*, 30 (5): 619–622.

Thompson, R. (1992) 'Developmental changes in research and risk benefit', in B. Stanley and J. Sieber (eds), *Social Research on Children and Adolescents: Ethical Issues*, London: Sage.

Thorne, B. (1993) *Gender Play: Girls and Boys in School*, Buckingham: Open University Press.

Trawick-Smith, J. (1998) 'School-based play and social interactions', in D.F. Fromberg and D. Bergen (eds), *Play from Birth to Twelve and Beyond*, New York: Garland.

Umek, L., Musek, P., Pecjak, S. and Kranjc, S. (1999) 'Symbolic play as a way of development and learning of pre-school children in pre-school institutions', *European Early Childhood Education Research Journal*, 7 (1): 35–44.

van Liempd, I. (2005) 'Making use of space: theory meets practice', *Children in Europe*, March, 16–17.

Van Oers, B. (1994) 'Semiotic activity of young children in play: the construction and use of schematic representations', *European Early Childhood Education Research Journal*, 2 (1): 19–33.

Vygotsky, L. (1978) *Mind in Society: The Development of Higher Psychological Processes*, Cambridge, MA: Harvard University Press.

Walkerdine, V. (1986) 'Progressive pedagogy and political struggle', *Screen*, 27 (5): 54–61.

Weber, M. (1949) *Economy and Society: An Outline of Interpretive Sociology*, Berkeley: University of California Press.

Wellman, H. (1990) *The Child's Theory of Mind*, London: MIT.

Wertsch, K.J.V. (1985) *Culture, Communication and Cognition: Vygotskian Perspectives*, Cambridge: Cambridge University Press.

White, F., Hargreaves, L. and Newbold, C. (1995) 'The midday playground experiences of five and six year-olds: mixed messages and neglected opportunities', *International Play Journal*, 3 (3): 153–167.

White, J. (2002) *The Child's Mind*, London: RoutledgeFalmer.

Willes, M. (1981) 'Children becoming pupils: a study of discourse in nursery and reception classes' in Adelman, C. (ed.), *Uttering, Muttering*, London: Grant McIntyre.

Winnicott, D.W. (1971) *Playing and Reality*, London: Routledge.

Wood, D. and Wood, H. (1996) 'Vygotsky, tutoring and learning', *Oxford Review of Education*, 22 (1): 5–16.

Wood, E. and Attfield, J. (2005) *Play, Learning and the Early Childhood Curriculum*, London: Paul Chapman.

Woodhead, M. (1989) '"School starts at five … or four years old?" the rationale for changing admission policies in England and Wales', *Journal of Educational Policy*, 4 (1): 1–21.

Woods, P., Boyle, M. and Hubbard, N. (1999) *Multicultural Children in the Early Years*, Clevedon: Multilingual Matters.

Yelland, N. (ed.) (1998) *Gender in Early Childhood*, London: Routledge.

Yelland, N. and Grieshaber, S. (1998) 'Blurring the Edges', in N. Yelland (ed.), *Gender in Early Childhood*, London: Routledge.

Index